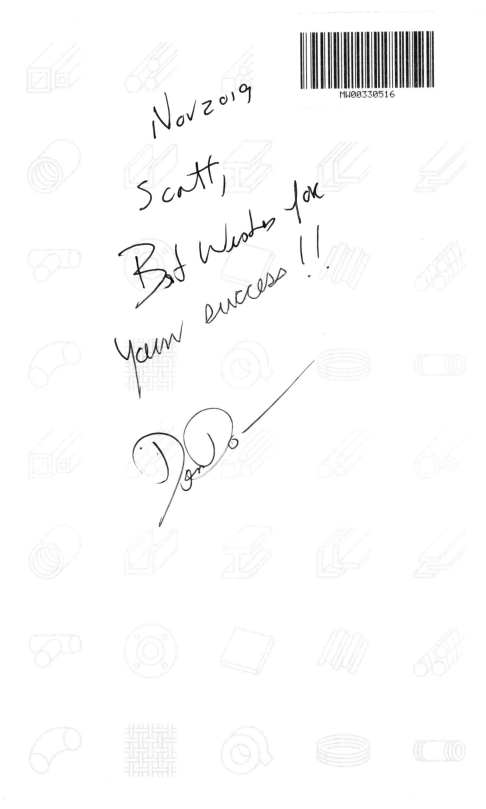

Nov 2019

Scott,

Best Wishes for
your success !!.

SOFT AS STEEL

Praise

"*Soft as Steel* provides tremendous insights and analysis that can serve as a guide not only for those in the construction industry, but for anyone in his or her day-to-day life interacting with others. Dennis's focus on the more intangible skills that accompany a good communicator and leader is a unique take for our industry that everyone could stand to benefit from. He also cites plenty of real-world examples, either from his own experiences or from his 'conversation partners,' that provide the reader with ample utility and value that will help them better engage with their clients, business partners, and employees."

Milo Riverso, Ph.D., P.E.
President and CEO
STV
New York, New York

"This book is the first, that I know of, to provide a self-help for soft skills specifically in the construction industry. Its conversational tone makes it an easy read. The tool itself will be invaluable to individuals who realize technical knowledge, skills, and abilities need to be supported by your own personal style, communication, and compassion to really get the job done."

Ann Marie Sweet-Abshire
Senior Executive
Federal Government
Washington, D.C.

"This writing truly captures the facts about the importance of soft skills, not only in the construction industry, but for everyday life as well. Combining real-life confirmations and dialogues from a variety of backgrounds and experience levels, the theme is beautifully illustrated to the reader in a way that is relatable for individuals ranging from entry-level positions on up to managerial and executive roles."

Cameron Geske
Project Manager
Construction Services Firm
Phoenix, Arizona

"Our company is growing fast. Soft skills are important as we maintain existing relationships and create new ones. The book *Soft as Steel* will help our team understand soft skill benefits, but more importantly, how to encourage soft skill behavior."

Sandy Hamby, FCMAA, AIA, CCM
President
MOCA Systems, Inc
San Antonio, Texas

"Throughout life, mentors provide guidance for each of us to grow. The first mentors were our parents, and later teachers, coaches, etc., nurtured our development. This book is a compilation of golden nuggets learned by many knowledgeable and successful people. Absorb these nuggets and use them to nurture your own development and success. This is essential reading for anyone who wants to excel in the construction industry."

Bob Swanson
Forty-five-year construction
industry thought leader
Minneapolis, Minnesota

"*Soft as Steel* highlights the paradox in the construction industry. Buildings are still built by people. Soft skills required!"

Shawn Mahoney
CEO
OAC Services
Seattle, Washington

SOFT

LEADERSHIP QUALITIES TO GROW RELATIONSHIPS

AS

AND SUCCEED IN BUSINESS AND LIFE

STEEL

∎ ∎ ∎

DENNIS DORAN

BOSS

MEDIA

Manufactured and printed in the United States of America

Distributed globally by Boss Media
New York | Los Angeles | London | Sydney

Print ISBN: 978-1-63337-327-3
E-book ISBN: 978-1-63337-328-0

Library of Congress Control Number: 2019949577

Printed in the United States of America

Contents

ACKNOWLEDGMENTS

I am grateful to all the folks who took time to have conversations with me and for their thoughts, words, phrases, and stories that you will learn and benefit from reading, reflecting on, and feeling. From them I gathered valuable insights into the subject of this book.

For a dear friend who provided the inspirational thought that launched this endeavor by saying, "What are you waiting for?"

For my sons, Alex and Christopher, whom I love deeply. Their caring for me brings me so much happiness.

For the "team" that helped me launch this first-in-my-lifetime endeavor as I strive to follow my calling—Michelle Borquez Robinson of BOSS Media, Sherrie Clark, and Michael Saltar.

Foreword

You know the stereotype of the typical construction industry professional: hard hat, khakis, steel-toed boots, clipboard, chin stubble (because the stereotype is male, of course), maybe a plug of chew in his jaw. With a grim, determined look on his face, he stands on a girder, high above the city, gazing out over his creation and says, "I build buildings; I don't do that people thing."

Like in any stereotype, there are individuals who fit that mold to a T. But if you look beyond the cartoonish trope, a very different reality emerges. First of all, more and more women are rising through the ranks to the top of the field, so there goes the chin stubble reference. But more to the point of this discussion, it turns out that the people thing, the so-called "soft stuff," isn't a touchy-feely distraction from the real work at all. It is, in fact, the fundamental core material that makes any project a success or failure. As Dennis Doran teaches us in this fantastic book, soft is anything but.

Personally, I'm not surprised. I've been writing, speaking, and consulting about Extreme Leadership—which has at its core the practice of cultivating Love—for twenty years. I've used a lot of words that have been traditionally written off as soft, squishy, kumbaya stuff by people who think of themselves as hard-core, no-nonsense business types in just about every kind of industry you can imagine. But those same people who once turned up their noses at these ideas, now freely recognize that the values of trust, love, integrity, and humanity are, in fact, hard-core business practices, too.

The challenge always comes down to how to apply these ideals and principles in ways that directly impact productivity, efficiency, safety, project management, and all the other critical, measurable results that construction professionals have to deliver every day.

Ultimately, to succeed in today's rapidly evolving construction landscape, an organization requires its management and labor force to be proficient in both hard and soft skills. Hard skills involve the mechanics of "doing the job," and soft skills are all about how the job gets done—the recognition of emotional intelligence, an understanding of the generational differences in a workforce, and a style of communication that drives stellar results.

For construction organizations, getting managers and employees to practice these so-called soft skills may at times seem impossibly hard. Enter Dennis Doran, who has been teaching this very thing to the construction industry for many years.

Although the fantastic ideas he offers herein apply to anyone in any kind of business, they are particularly focused on the construction field, and for good reason: it's Dennis's area of experience and expertise. He has drawn not only from his own work with countless professionals, but on myriad of fresh, new interviews with leaders in the field—from management and unions alike. It's rare to find a body of work that is simultaneously inspirational and practical, tried-and-true and innovative, conventionally wise and packed with original research. Well, you hold that rarity in your hands right now, so please don't squander the opportunity to learn from the best in your field.

You may still be wondering if the ideas in this book really are, when all is said and done, too soft for your rough-and-tumble world?

Well... let me put it to you this way, my friend: yes, they're soft.

Soft as steel.

And if you're ready to do the hard work of the soft stuff, you'll build success beyond your wildest imagination. No hard hat or steel-toed boots required.

—**Steve Farber**
Author of *Love Is Just Damn Good Business*,
Founder and CEO,
The Extreme Leadership Institute,
San Diego, California

Preface

My goal is to give you tools that you can use to learn, apply what you learned, and be inspired to be a better you for yourself and for the people in your life. This book will help you learn so much about yourself—more than you think or feel there is to know right now. It will help you measure your soft skills, moving you higher and further in your life's journey in our great industry and everywhere else.

The book is organized into five parts. Part 1, "Building Your Foundation," is where you will begin to learn about yourself. Here you will complete an activity designed to identify the twelve qualities that are the most important to you for a happy life before you go forward into the remainder of the book. You will do this by completing a series of forced rankings, the same activity that all the folks whom you will hear from in the pages of this book completed. I call these folks my "conversation partners."

I will tell you what I learned from the conversations themselves, and wherever I can, I'll use the words and stories of my conversation partners. I'll also indicate the generation of the conversation partner (baby boomers: 1946–1964, Generation X: 1965–1980, millennials: 1981–1995) to give you a little more information, so that you can make a more personal connection with the thoughts and stories you will read.

In Part 2, "The Most Frequently Mentioned Soft Skills," I will present the results of the survey from the conversation partners and discuss their most frequently mentioned qualities. I hope that Part 2 will be bookmarked by you for your future and regular review. You can also compare your own survey results from Part 1, focusing particularly on those that match. Keep in mind that all the qualities included in the survey are important and that this survey is only the beginning of what you can learn about soft skills.

Part 3 is called "Nuts, Bolts, and Some Great Thoughts," and it contains a collection of phrases and thoughts that were inspired by talking with my conversation partners. These are just darn-good, practical ways of reminding you how important soft skills are. I hope you will enjoy reading them and using them to start other conversations.

I'm calling Part 4 "Do It Yourself." In this part of the book, I will talk with you about the most basic, most significant, and most underappreciated skill and process—communication. By the time you arrive in this part of the book, you will have read a lot about communication. Communication is something you do every day, from the time you wake up until the time you fall asleep. Oh, and yes, some of us even do it while we are asleep. Regardless, if you are like most of us, you could probably benefit from improving how you communicate.

You will also have the opportunity to take three quick assessments to gather some facts about you that will be really helpful for getting a simple, informative understanding of yourself to build into your own Soft Skills Personal Improvement Plan. You will find some guidance and suggestions for building your plan in Part 4.

Finally, in Part 5, "Recommended Reading and Other Resources," I'll share with you a few books and other resources I encourage you to include in your Soft Skills Personal Improvement Plan.

My Inspiration

Over ten years ago, I finally learned that there was, and continues to be, a plan for me, and all I need to do is let the plan unfold. Shortly after, I read a book that changed my view on *everything* about living. That book is *The Radical LEAP*, written by my good friend and mentor, Steve Farber. I didn't know it at the time, but my plan was unfolding, and I was at the beginning of understanding what soft skills were and that I had a passion for helping other folks learn about them. But of course, I still made bad decisions and didn't listen to my own voice.

I have had a long career in the construction industry and thought of myself as successful there. It wasn't until I got fired from a job for the very first time that I woke up and realized that my calling was to help people in the construction industry become more successful by talking, teaching, motivating, and inspiring them about the role of soft skills in our industry and lives.

Since then, I have thought about what I need to have in the front of my mind to guide me, and I always fall back on the words I read in that book in 2010: "Do what you love in the service of people who love what you do." I've been following that guidance every day since. This book is a result of that work, and I hope you love it!

Introduction

What Is This Book About?

oft as Steel will help leaders at all levels of experience, responsibility, and those in all roles within the construction industry and elsewhere to understand the fundamental, vital importance of a person's soft skills. The book's title conveys the truth that soft skills are for people what steel is to so many structures—essential to building something strong that will last for a long time. Soft skills are the difference maker for people; they are the qualities that are essential to building and maintaining relationships with people in all parts of their lives.

In the pages of this book, I will share with you the results of a series of over thirty conversations I was privileged to have. I held these interviews with leaders in the construction industry like you, seeking to understand their perspective about soft skills—what's important about them, how leaders think that people see them, and why we should be talking about them.

You will read in-depth about ten of the most frequently mentioned qualities throughout these conversations. These qualities were mentioned repeatedly, and you will see that several of my conversation partners discuss them. I'll also touch on ten additional high-ranking qualities to round out the top twenty.

I will also discuss fifty-two thoughts that were inspired by these conversations, which you can use to help you pause and reflect on the practical importance of your own soft skills. Finally, included in these pages are activities and planning exercises that will benefit you.

The Conversation Partners

You will learn about soft skills through the experiences of my conversation partners, people who are leaders in the construction industry spanning three generations. They are project owners, contractors, subcontractors, engineers, construction managers, and representatives of building trade unions. You will hear them talk about what soft skills are, which are the most important to them, and the role these soft skills played in their success. They will share stories that will help you understand that soft skills are important to everything you do, and at the same time, why they are often hard to learn. Their experiences explain in simple and personal terms why these soft skills or qualities of people in the construction industry have a direct, measurable impact on both personal and professional success. These leaders will talk about what individual soft skills mean to them and share their experiences related to each.

Why Is This Book So Important?

It is not enough to be good at doing the job. That's about hard skills—knowledge, skills, and abilities. It is my goal to help good people like you reach your fullest potential by focusing on your soft skills. It doesn't matter whether you are in the first year or so of your career in construction or have thirty years of experience. Better is still better.

This book will talk about "how we are" is more important than "who we are." I didn't hear the words "soft skills" until just a few years ago, although I had heard of "people skills" and "communication skills." I never took a class at any level of my education or construction career that taught me about soft skills. We only learned a little about managing, supervising, and leading people. Mostly we talked about getting the job done.

These days, we are talking more and more about how much is changing in the construction industry and how much harder it is to get the job done. Anything we can do to improve our abilities to get and complete jobs must be considered. Soft skills are a bigger and bigger part of that.

We are in a place in time where the interactions among different generations, personal values, and varying needs are placing an incredible demand on our efficiency. The qualities of a person are more important than ever before. Diversity in our workforce doesn't just mean diversity in gender, race, or ethnicity. It also relates to values and qualities of people. For example, your level of emotional intelligence is fundamental to your life's happiness and success, yet most in our industry don't have a clue about what emotional intelligence is and how it relates to you and your soft skills.

Soft skills aren't really skills at all. They are the qualities, attributes, and behaviors that help you be a better person to work with or work for. They make you someone people will want to do business with and a person with whom people will want to build a relationship. That sounds like something worth learning about, doesn't it?

Historically, the construction industry has not valued soft skills. We did not recognize the significant role soft skills play in the success of each of us individually and collectively as owners, contractors, subcontractors, architects, engineers, suppliers, members of building trade unions, etc. Soft skills directly impact the bottom line of any business. You may be a first-year apprentice just learning a trade, a student in class learning about job-cost estimating, or the CEO of a global construction firm. It doesn't really matter. You will benefit greatly from learning more about soft skills from construction leaders just like you.

That's why this book is so important! I am going to share conversations I had with a wide cross-section of folks in our industry so that you will understand how to maximize your potential as well as better understand the people in your life at work, in your community, and at home.

BUILDING

YOUR

FOUNDATION

What Soft Skills Are Important to You?

Let's begin building your foundation of understanding about soft skills with an activity that will take you about fifteen minutes to complete.

Before I talked with my conversation partners about soft skills, I asked them to complete a survey to learn the personality qualities they believe have been the most important in their working life's journey. As you complete this exercise, your instruction is the same. Keep the work setting in mind as you complete it.

There are four groups of words on each of the next few pages. The words describe a person's soft skills: their habits, qualities, and attributes.

If you are not sure of a word's meaning, take a moment and google it. I do this often. :)

Please follow the instructions for each word group, one to four, in order. All you have to do is force rank each group of words.

After completing each group, proceed to "Your Final Ranking" and follow the instructions to determine your final list of the twelve qualities most important to you in your working career.

Do Your Own Ranking of Qualities

GROUP 1

Please force rank these qualities from 1 to 10, with 1 being the most important to you and 10 being the least important to you. Simply enter the number in the box next to each word.

	Adaptable
	Ambitious
	Attentive
	Authentic
	Calming
	Candid
	Careful
	Caring
	Confident
	Good Communicator

GROUP 2

Please force rank these qualities from 1 to 10 with 1 being the most important to you and 10 being the least important to you. Simply enter the number in the box next to each word.

	Quality
	Charismatic
	Creative
	Dedicated
	Empathetic
	Energetic
	Ethical
	Flexible
	Good Listener
	Hard Working
	Honest

GROUP 3

Please force rank these qualities from 1 to 10 with 1 being the most important to you and 10 being the least important to you. Simply enter the number in the box next to each word.

	Inclusive
	Influential
	Inspiring
	Integrity
	Motivating
	Passionate
	Patient
	Persuasive
	Positive
	Practical

GROUP 4

Please force rank these qualities from 1 to 10 with 1 being the most important to you and 10 being the least important to you. Simply enter the number in the box next to each word.

	Reasonable
	Relationship Builder
	Self-Aware
	Sense of Humor
	Sensible
	Sensitive
	Sincere
	Trustworthy
	Visionary
	Warm

YOUR FINAL RANKING

Enter the qualities you ranked 1, 2, and 3 from Groups 1-4 in the righthand column.

Force rank these qualities from 1 to 12 with 1 being the most important to you and 12 being the least important.

I hope you find your results interesting. I think it will help you appreciate even more what this book is about, and you will come back to your results in Part 4.

What I Learned from the Conversations: Soft Skills and What They Are

Maybe it's as simple as saying that soft skills are your personal qualities, traits, and characteristics, or maybe your personality. I don't know about you, but these kinds of vague phrases leave the door wide open so you're never able to get a handle on what soft skills are, which would allow you to have an opportunity to improve yourself. My experience in our industry is that most folks think about soft skills in relation to communication only. That may be how you think about what they are. That's not wrong, but there's a lot more to soft skills than that.

Let's look at the challenge of understanding what soft skills really are. I think you will appreciate the words of one of the boomers who said this:

"Soft skills are the characteristics that everybody needs to negotiate properly through a conversation, through an idea, through a concept, to get your point across, to develop dialogue, and ultimately to get some sort of resolution or answer.

"Soft skills are the things that you can't put your finger on, that you can't learn in a book. They are hard to paint because they require some

> ...MOST FOLKS THINK ABOUT SOFT SKILLS IN RELATION TO COMMUNICATION ONLY.... THERE'S A LOT MORE TO SOFT SKILLS THAN THAT."

experience, and things like that you don't always learn from a course or a book. They're hard to grasp."

This person's way of expressing what soft skills are sounds a bit confusing, at least to me. The confusion makes the case for the value of a straightforward and practical discussion about soft skills, which is why I wrote this book.

I heard this very full description from a Gen Xer:

"To me, soft skills translate to your ability to connect, inspire, and motivate people. It's the ability to listen effectively and communicate in a way that helps get action and results in the direction that you are trying to head.

"Soft skills are not easily taught, but they can be modeled. They can be developed over the years. Some come more naturally to people [than others]. But I do believe you can coach soft skills in individuals.

"I look back on my own career. There are individuals who were mentors to me on a lot of levels—technical knowledge, an understanding of how the business works and the different angles, and the different entities involved and what their motivations are. With a lot of the great mentors I had, it wasn't just about me paying attention to the technical knowledge they were conveying, but it was also learning their techniques and strategies to effectively drive to a positive result.

"Some of those techniques were largely [centered] around how they communicated, how they listened, how they repeated information to ensure the interaction they were having with others was effective and positive, how they found ways to get to common ground, especially in situations that were more difficult, where people are in their separate camps or opinions on what outcome they wanted. You need to find a way to get to common ground. Soft skills are a key part of that. When you watch others closely and can observe and try to take that in, it helps you think about how you could also effect change in similar ways. You won't do it the same way. Hopefully, you do it in a way that has evolved or progressed for yourself personally."

This individual covers a lot of ground in his statement. You see that this person touches on the fact that soft skills are about things other than the technical or hard skills you do in your job. The way communication is discussed is right on target, and we'll talk about this in more detail later in this book.

Another thought this individual shared that is very helpful in thinking about where you are in your career path is the importance of a mentor and the difference one can make. No matter where you are in your construction career, if you haven't worked with a mentor yet, now's the time.

A boomer says it this way:

"[Soft skills are] the skill to communicate, the skill to relate to people, the skill to listen to people, and the ability to work with different personalities in any given situation. They're all teachable, some by classroom and lectures and some by example and relationships through mentoring and developing experience in the workplace."

You see that communication is important, including the specific mention of listening. Listening is a skill that can be practiced and improved upon. It's the most important element in communication, and it serves at least two valuable purposes: one, while you are listening, you are showing interest in and focusing on the value of the other person as a human being, and two, listening is the way you get to know the person with whom you are communicating. When you listen well, you will then be able to say the right thing in the situation so the other person can get to know you.

Another Xer said:

"To me, soft skills are those interpersonal communication skills that are probably somewhat underutilized, maybe undervalued, but they are the cohesiveness, the skill sets you have that can keep everything together. Really, when used effectively, soft skills can help you accomplish your mission without having to come off as playing the authoritative dictator role. Instead,

you are trying to work with everybody and their different communication styles and personalities to accomplish your goals and your vision."

This Xer highlights why it is important for us to talk about soft skills—they are underutilized and undervalued. Your qualities are visible to others in your actions and your words, and you need to always be mindful of this. A millennial put it this way:

"I would say you don't learn [soft] skills in college, but [they] have to be nurtured just as well as the technical knowledge that you do begin to learn in college or with schooling."

Remember that soft skills are not the same as hard skills, and they are not so easy to define. Many soft skills are really qualities, attributes, and behaviors of people.

> ...EVERY JOB, WHATEVER THE JOB IS, IS AN OPPORTUNITY TO BE OF SERVICE TO SOMEONE.."

You can see that it can be confusing to talk about the differences between soft skills and hard skills. For the purposes of this book, hard skills are about the things you do at your job, the things that get you in the game, get you qualified to be able to perform a job. In our industry, it starts with schooling for the job, apprenticeships for the trades, and college for engineers, architects, and construction managers.

Someone who understands the value of soft skills never thinks about just performing the job. I know that each and every job, whatever the job is, is an opportunity to be of service to someone. It is an opportunity to connect on a deeper level, which leads to deeper success. That's why soft skills are so important to be aware of, care about, and value.

How you are is vital to your success at work and elsewhere. What people see and hear from you and what you see and hear from every person in your life is what produces lasting relationships. You're not just a contractor. You don't just build stuff. You're not just an engineer. You don't just design things. You aren't just an apprentice, journeyperson, mechanic, or glazer. First and foremost, you are a person, relating to other people.

Your soft skills are so important in everything you do. They will set you apart and provide you with opportunities to grow and succeed. That's why you need to know what soft skills are.

What I Learned from the Conversations: Emotional Intelligence

By now you have a better understanding of what soft skills are and how important they are to you in all your relationships. One of the primary soft skill areas I encourage you to understand more about is emotional intelligence, or EQ. Unfortunately, my conversations with leaders in the industry confirmed that a lot of folks aren't familiar with the term "emotional intelligence." Think of emotional intelligence as the ability to be able to answer two questions: first, how much do you know about your own emotions, and second, how much do you know about other people's emotions?

A lot has been written about emotional intelligence, and it fits well within the discussion about soft skills. If you think for just a moment about how your workday goes when you are in a bad mood or someone you work with is having a bad day, what you are talking about here is how emotion impacts behavior. All people, including you, have emotions. Simply put, our brains are wired so that emotions affect our ability to think and act rationally. A lot of us are overcontrolled by our emotions, and when you understand this, you can do something about it.

One of the most practical books on this topic is *Emotional Intelligence 2.0* by Travis Bradberry and Jean Greaves. This book teaches us that your emotional intelligence is about competence and skills—personal competence and social competence. Personal competence involves two skills—self-awareness and self-management. Social competence also involves two skills—social awareness and relationship management. Your emotional intelligence is in play all the time, balancing all of these competencies and skills.

Every one of your soft skills is affected by your emotions. As I said earlier, humans are emotional and many of us are more controlled by our emotions than we would like. To be more successful in all your relationships, it is important to understand something about emotional intelligence. You don't want to be one of those folks about whom people say, "He's really good at the technical or hard skills part of his job, but he's difficult to get along with."

Think about emotional intelligence as one of the soft skills areas you need to understand in order to get better results in all that you do with others. Start by looking at yourself and your emotions. It all starts with that look in the mirror and then expands by paying careful attention to what's going on with the other people around you.

A boomer said it very well:

"I would say emotional intelligence is that inner core in us, what makes us tick. We have to understand that first before we relate to others. If we haven't delved into who we are, it's difficult to understand where other people are coming from. The first thing is [to develop] an understanding of yourself. It's those inner things, what makes you tick, your emotions, your values, who you are, and an understanding of who you are, and then the acceptance of that. Sometimes we are in denial. That also makes it hard to understand other people."

You can improve this part of how you are. Your success in relationships is about how you manage your emotions and being aware of others' emotions so that you get the best results when you are talking to people. Your success is more than just knowing more or being smarter, more than just being good with the tools of your trade or profession.

What I Learned from the Conversations: Soft Skills and Why They Matter

Some things bear repeating, and the answer to this question is certainly one of these things. Read the words from five people representing three primary generations in our industry as they answer why soft skills matter. All five of them say it with conviction using different words and from their different perspectives and roles in our industry. So, here's why soft skills matter...

A baby boomer said:

"I think you have to [talk about soft skills] because the world has changed. When you and I were younger, when I was in the trade... feelings weren't a part of construction. The foreman told you what to do. If you didn't do it, you would go home. That worked for that time frame. It worked when I was growing up. You accepted that. But certainly, as we evolved, as the construction industry evolved, that no longer became acceptable. A lot of the things that were done and how they were done are totally unaccept-able today. If you want to attract the people we are hoping to attract—wom-en and minorities who come from different cultures and backgrounds—we have to be aware of how what we say is interpreted by them. It's a tough world out there in terms of recruiting people to come into our trade. When you get someone interested in the trade, you don't want to offend him/her by something you say, because that is stupid. You want to accommodate. You have to accommodate in today's world. We don't have the people com-ing to us in the masses to fill these jobs. Also, you can't be as belligerent as we were back then.

"It's no longer the old boys' club. It can't be. There are girls here. There are minorities. We are all minorities at some point. You have to accommodate. People are moving around the world and changing where they live. We have to be a little more sensitive in how we act and what we say, especially. Soft skills are a big part of that. It's something that is so important. We have one chance to make a first impression. If you don't have the ability, or at least the smarts, to step back and think before you speak, you could offend a lot of people very quickly."

As you just finished reading this last quote, I want to remind you that all the quoted content is as spoken. I'm mentioning this because this baby boomer speaks in very direct terms using words that may seem "not so soft." If you are in the first years of your career in the construction industry, the view from this person's long career in our industry is genuine and captures a lot of why soft skills are so important. This person is describing change in a pretty persuasive way.

A Gen Xer said:

"… it's the soft skills that enable someone to move up in their career and deal with subcontractors and deal with the owner. You can have a guy who knows everything there is to know about concrete and masonry and this and that. If they don't have soft skills and they don't know [how] to sit in front of the subcontractor or owner and talk to them and work with them, it's not a good situation."

Another Gen Xer brings the changes in how we interact in our industry into the discussion:

"… we definitely need to [talk about soft skills] from the perspective that the biggest challenge in construction is communication. In the past, you just relied on people to get stuff done because the blueprints show it, and we were trusting that our crews could analyze and organize it. I would say we haven't done it as efficiently as we could. If we could harness the

ability to communicate more effectively, whether it's through technology (or another way), that is one piece of it.

"But the other piece is being able to inspire the team, create a sense of trust on the team, and being able to communicate effectively to get stuff done. Being authoritarian and doing the bully pulpit stuff works to a degree, but I don't think it pulls out all the proficiency that can happen with the talent of people we have today. More importantly, if we don't have better soft skills, people won't want to be in this business any longer. The days of 'we're just going to get that job, shut our mouths, show up from nine to five, work our eight hours, punch the clock and go home,' people don't want to do that anymore. At least the best ones don't. Our business won't stick around if we continue to operate that way. I think the best leaders know that. I think people are doing it to a degree but maybe haven't defined it as soft skills training. I think the more awareness we have about the potential that each person can bring is just communicated better. If you work on those skills, it can bring a lot out in people you didn't know had it in them."

A third Gen Xer said it this way:

"Possessing effective soft skills can result in improved outcomes. The more individuals improve their soft skills, regardless of their role—whether they are jobsite foremen, superintendents, project managers—having better soft skills and better listening skills and better outcome-focused communication has a direct impact on the ability to deliver projects better. If individuals can pause and try to improve their soft skills, being aware and trying are the first steps. You have the ability to try to get better project outcomes, which is what the industry needs. We are not currently good at evolving. Without good communication and soft skills and acknowledgment of one another and the assets and benefits each party brings to the table, you can't get there. It's important to talk about what soft skills are and to try to help all workforces. I don't care if you're in a trade or are a professional. All workforces need to have positive soft skills. As humans, we need to have

positive soft skills. *Culturally, unfortunately, some sides of our business leave some of those skills at home. We shouldn't.*"

Here's the way a millennial nails the people part of everything we do in construction:

"*[Soft skills matter] because things get built through relationships, through people liking you. Everybody has the hard skills. Everybody can get on a computer, paint a wall, and operate a forklift. Everybody has those. But it takes the people who connect on a human level with others, who really step it up and first of all sell work, manage the work, maintain the emotions and attitudes. The world is changing.*

"*I know I'm young, and in general, I may be stereotyped as a millennial, which I am. I see the world changing daily and the cultures and people. It's not the way it was back then, even though I really wasn't around back then. You have to be a people person. It's the same way with a server in a restaurant. Yeah, she can pour your drinks and bring you food. So can the rest of us. If she's nice and tends to you and talks to you and makes you laugh, she earns more.*"

I'd say these five folks make the case very well. I'm sure you can relate to one or more of them. Knowing yourself and getting to know others is the difference maker in our business and relationships. This is why developing and using your soft skills is so important. These conversation partners all tell you that the reasons we need to be talking about soft skills touch every aspect of our business, community, and personal interactions.

And, if you still need convincing, here's a "boots-on-the-ground" answer from another Gen Xer:

"*I think the construction industry traditionally has lacked soft skills. The last ten to fifteen years, that's changed a bit. That's evolved. We see people not just as yellers and screamers anymore. I think in order to get things done in a market like right now where we are incredibly busy, the soft skills are so much more important than being able to pick up the phone and threaten people to get stuff done."*

What I Learned from the Conversations: Self-Perception and How You See Yourself

Self-perception is all about looking in the mirror because how you see yourself is the most important ingredient in your foundation. Another term used to describe this fundamental and important part of your foundation is "self-awareness." We'll talk more about this, give you some additional tasks to do, and hopefully, you will grasp this firmly as you work through your own Soft Skills Personal Improvement Plan in Part 4.

Take a minute and answer the question I asked all the folks I talked with:

If I were to ask someone who had known you for several years how they would describe you, what would they say?

_____

_____

_____

_____

_____

_____

_____

_____

Was it hard to answer this question? How do you really know what people would say? One thought that this brings into focus is that you need to look at yourself honestly. If you do, then there's a good chance your view and the other person's view will connect. If they don't, focus on the differences and try to learn why there are differences. Keep in mind that your soft skills are seen by others in your actions and your words.

Now let's look at how several of my conversation partners expressed themselves in answering the question you just answered.

"I think they would describe me as hardworking and driven. I think people would describe me as, I hope, a warm or good communicator. I can meet people easily and talk with people and engage with people. I think that I am honest and transparent. I would say that my soft skills are probably better than my technical skills."

"… straightforward and intelligent and analytical. I am a caring person."

"A very caring individual. He is honest, has high integrity. His word is his bond. He will try his best to do whatever he says he has indicated verbally. You can count on him."

"Fair. Probably more middle of the road. Don't get too low, and don't get too high. Even-grounded. Even-keeled."

"Energetic and passionate. Hardworking. I would like to think honest and forthright. Some people would think I might be a bit fast (I don't know if that's the right word), but a quick-paced individual. Some who work for me may say demanding. I think they would also say committed to the cause, whatever the cause is, and willing to jump in the trenches with everyone around me because I care."

"Approachable. I think real, authentic, genuine, empathetic, caring about others, valuing other people's input and their opinions as well."

"… passionate and competitive are good words to use. I feel like whatever I'm doing, I try to be the best at it. I really always care about what I'm doing. Sometimes that can be a bad thing, but a lot of times, that's a

good thing. I think people would say I am very detailed in certain facets, especially work."

"I would say passionate, a good listener, willing to help out wherever needed, always willing to learn, dedicated."

"... softer than I was thirty years ago."

The last phrase brings a smile to my face. I've known this person, a boomer, for a long time. In just a few words, this person is talking about one of the realities that many folks struggle with—change. The book *Mindset* by Carol Dweck says that people can change many aspects of how they are—if they want to—by having a growth mindset. You can improve your soft skills. We'll talk more about mindset later in Part 4.

What I Learned from the Conversations: Important People in Your Life

All of us can point to one or more people we have known in our lives who were very important to our life's journey. If you haven't thought about this, I encourage you to take a few minutes and do it. For some of you, it may be a teacher or a coach from when you were very young. I've been humbled by hearing from a parent of a child I coached in a sport at the elementary school level. They reminded me of something I had taught their son that was very important to them, something they hadn't forgotten. If you take a few moments and think back over your career, you will surely find someone who was very important to you.

While you're reading how several of my conversation partners discussed the importance of other people in their lives, notice how they all talk about the person they are remembering by describing qualities this person had, what the relationship was like, and how knowing the person helped them develop.

This baby boomer told me about a person in their working life:

"[He was a] very caring individual. Honest. He wanted people to succeed and wanted to give people opportunities. He delighted in seeing people
rise to levels they didn't think they could go. He loved to encourage people
and give them opportunities. He had some interesting characteristics. He
wouldn't tell you what to do, but he would give you nudges so that it was
pretty clear what he had in mind.

"I never wanted to disappoint him. I tried to exceed his expectations. He
was your cheerleader. He was there wanting you to exceed his expectations.
His expectations were always realistic. Sometimes you thought they were
beyond your capabilities, but they were realistic.

"He was humble. He didn't take credit. He gave credit to those whom
he led, almost to a fault. If he had a weakness, he was open about that.
He surrounded himself with people who could overcome his weakness and
had strengths. He was more than willing to delegate responsibility. It wasn't
about him. It was about the team, so to speak. Very honest. What he told
you was real. It was refreshing to work for somebody like that."

Another baby boomer talked about an important person in his
career with whom he worked for a long time:

"He trusted me. He had confidence in me. He allowed me to get into
positions of authority and provided a safety net without dictating what I
should do. In other words, he let me learn and guided me rather than told
me what to do.

"He had qualities that were and remain important to me. He did what
he said he was going to do. He stood his own ground when he needed to.
Agreed to disagree. I call it a leader. But that is because he had the attributes I value. He modeled the qualities. There was no class. There was no
'let me teach you this.' It was watching what he did, interacting with him,
watching how he interacted with others."

A millennial talked about a person he worked with on one of
his first projects:

"They had a lot of experience. The knowledge they brought to the table came through experience, not education, [through] their ability to communicate. I don't know how to say this. Their physical appearance? Their presence? They opened me up to how to communicate with different people. Certainly, working down where I am in North Carolina, it's much different than in the Washington, D.C., area. Communicating with people who were born and raised and live here and make a living here are different to deal with. Helping me communicate with people from a different part of the country has helped me a lot."

This story is a terrific one to help you see that your soft skills and those of others involve communication—that skill that is basic to your ability to get to know people and to help people get to know you. Are you keeping track of how many times and in what ways communication is coming up? Hmm.

A Gen Xer told me about a friend who has become a business colleague:

"He was thoughtful and smart and supportive of me. He was a good listener. He was engaging. He asked questions. I don't mean that in a random sense, but I found that this person is always asking questions like 'How are you doing?' or 'How can I help you?' or 'What challenges are you dealing with?' Whatever path you're choosing, he is there to support you. Honest. Will give you honest feedback. It doesn't mean that honest feedback is there for me to evaluate. He never impresses upon a fact that he thinks this is how you should do it. He is just there as a resource, as a sounding board to help you work through what your particular issue or challenge may be."

So, now you can see that there are important people in your life everywhere. Before we go on, take a few minutes and use the space below to say something about a person in your life who was or is important to you:

PART

2

THE MOST
FREQUENTLY
MENTIONED
SOFT SKILLS

The survey I asked folks to complete produced very interesting results. Although it identified each partner's top twelve qualities, when we discussed the results together, I asked each of them to only tell me what their top four qualities meant to them. I also asked them to tell me a story that illustrated how the quality was important in a situation or during a period in their lives. I didn't ask them to define the words they used to identify these qualities but instead checked the Merriam-Webster Online Dictionary for definitions. The definitions are helpful because when you read what

■

43

the word means, it produces an understanding to which you will relate. The individual stories will really help you understand what the quality is all about in a real-life way.

There are five qualities that are very closely connected: trustworthy, honest, integrity, ethical, and authentic. If you think about what they mean to you, it is difficult to think about them in isolation. By that I mean that these qualities overlap and support each other, and where you find one, you tend to find the others.

Top Ten Qualities

Here's what I learned about the ten most frequently mentioned qualities among all of the conversation partners, beginning with the five that are really closely connected to each other.

1. **Trustworthy**—worthy of confidence: dependable

The definition is a practical expression of what this quality is. A millennial said this:

"Something that was told to me early on in my career is the only thing you have going into any situation is your word, unless you have a reason for the person not to believe you or trust you. Being trustworthy is something you earn over time by demonstrating that you can be trusted and that you act in a genuine manner and an ethical manner consistently.

"If you have built trust with an individual and you tell them something they may not like to hear or don't necessarily agree with, they tend to be more reasonable. It opens people to listen to what you're saying instead of figuring out a way to counter your stance."

A baby boomer offered this, along with a story:

"Trustworthy means that people will trust you. You won't do something to harm them. They can rely upon what you said. They can rely upon the information you gave them. They won't get hurt.

"Early in my career, I was called into the office of the head of the firm I worked for. He said to me, 'I want you to diagnose this problem on a project.' The project was a very visible public facility. The mayor wanted it to open in time for his primaries. I went out to the project and diagnosed it. I called the boss with my diagnosis of the problem. Based upon my diagnosis, he let go of the staff that was causing the issue and left me out there and told me to take over the job and get it done by the time I said I could get it done by. And I did. He trusted me."

Another boomer talked about the quality of trustworthy beginning with his background starting in the trades. It is a very interesting and personal way of telling us what this quality means.

"It means a couple of things actually. If you say something to me, and you say it's between you and me, I wouldn't go against somebody's word and repeat it. If you trust me to be there at a certain time, I'll be there at a certain time. If you're trusting me to handle whatever business or commitment it may be, you can trust the fact I'll get it done to the best of my ability. I will not disappoint whoever I promised that I would take care of it.

"People have to be able to depend upon [you], if it's getting the job done, if it's picking somebody up at a certain time, if it's meeting somebody at a certain place, if it's saying, 'I'll help you in coaching' from a Little League standpoint to an adult. I think it's important because trust to me is something based on history. It's like respect where it has to be earned. It can't be something that's just given out.

"What I could probably relate [this to] in a bigger picture would be working out of town where you have to be there at a certain time on a Monday. The crew is depending on you. The company is depending on you. There is no excuse. You have to be there. You give yourself enough

time to check weather conditions, road conditions, and make appropriate changes. If you say you're going to be there at a certain time, you will be a little earlier than what you said. That is one phase of it.

"The other would be that you go into a jobsite. The owner is trusting you with his business that you will get the job done for him. You will do exactly what the job is calling for. In the industry, trust is something that [means] you have to know your folks are going to be there. It may be a crew that is depending on it. The end user is expecting it done. The owner is expecting it done. A lot of people are trusting the fact—it may be your skill level, it may be your personality, but you will represent them properly and get the job done right. It's part of my upbringing for me, carried it through my life, through my military career to the jobsite. It's something that's been instilled from an early age."

A millennial explained trustworthy with a story we can easily relate to:

"Being able to rely on someone. Not having doubts and being able to give someone a task or a responsibility. Knowing that they'll carry it out and bring up any concerns or questions they may have.

"Trust is everything to me. It's one of the main building blocks in life. If you don't have trust, you don't have anything. I rely heavily on trusting people. I trust them until they show me differently. I treat those people the same way. If I have an issue, I will tell them and not continue to lie or give them a preachy answer where it could be worse. Having that open communication and trust between people is huge.

"There was a previous project. Material wasn't ordered on my side. I had dropped the ball. They had put their trust in me to get everything there. I had completely forgotten. It was going to be a couple of weeks out. Rather than just letting them hang on a limb and saying, 'They'll be here,' I said, 'I dropped the ball. They're going to be here in two weeks. That's the best I can do.' Down the line, that gave them a sense of who I was and that I was going to tell them the truth—not just what *they wanted to hear, but the right answer. That took me a long way with the superintendent on that project. My honesty earned his trust."*

It's probably easy to see why this quality was the most frequently mentioned. There's a close connection between this quality and several others. You could say that if you are viewed by others as being trustworthy, a wide range of other qualities are present and appreciated by the people in your work life and personal life.

2. Honest—free from fraud or deception: legitimate, truthful

Let's start with a simple explanation and a good story in the words of a boomer:

"Telling the truth every day. Giving people the good news and the bad news. Being fair with people. It's something that hopefully comes naturally to people. As you know, sometimes that just doesn't happen. I need to give people the bad news along with the good news. Don't hold things back.

"We recently had a headquarters tenant who was getting ready to move into a new space. We could make the schedule. We could get them in, but they were not going to be happy. We were honest about it and had a good, frank discussion that, 'Yes, we will get the certificate of occupancy, and we will get you in the space, but your executives should have a "Wow!" when they move into this space. They will be disappointed with where we are.'

"We agreed to push the move back a couple of weeks and get it right. Nobody fought about it. Nobody threatened liquidated damages. We didn't ask for additional general conditions. It was just being honest and telling people what to expect. Giving the bad news now so we can give them the good news later on."

This next boomer's dialogue is very frank, and you will feel everything he has to say:

"Don't b**ls**t people. If there is something that has to be said, you have to say it respectfully. If you go into somebody's house, you're not going to steal anything from them. You're not going to abuse anything they may have. If you're honest with people, I think it's a huge trait where it all builds into the respect, the trust portion. I think that's an important skill that somebody has to have because there are people on jobsites, people in life, relatives, who may not be honest. They might be talking out of both sides of their mouth. I think honesty, if you develop that, and people trust that you're honest, it may be selling something, it may be with a customer on a jobsite, you're telling them exactly what's taking place, that you'll take care of it. It goes back into that trust piece: that you'll get it done.

"When you go onto a jobsite, in most cases in the glazing world, you are given a series of power tools to use. Some guys believe that to steal them is part of the process. To me, that wasn't worth me losing a job over. I know if I ever asked a contractor if I could borrow whatever tool he had, he would probably lend it to me. If I was dishonest and stole it and said it was lost on a jobsite, my integrity as a person, I lose that, and people tend to cast a shadow of doubt after a while. Being honest with people, not just in society but being honest on a jobsite, is huge, and it plays a major role in the success of us as union members. There are multiple tools spread around jobsites. If it's not yours, you leave it alone. You don't take it. If it's not nailed down, that does not mean it's yours.

"Being honest with guys on a crew is important. [I had] situations when I was working as the apprenticeship coordinator, taking some young folks and pulling them aside and giving them that 'come-to-Jesus' speech: 'You're slipping up'; 'You're sliding'; 'You're falling down, and you need to do this to get back on track.' Sometimes it works. Sometimes it doesn't. You can't save everybody. It's important that people be in that honest circle and that people know when they come to you, you *will give them an honest answer. You will be honest in who you are as a person."*

I don't think this person missed a thing. His way of expressing what honest means is so powerful. Having qualities like honesty may seem obvious, but that doesn't mean we get the fundamental importance of this or any quality that seems so simple. When we are talking about how people behave, it is never simple.

A Gen Xer:

"Honesty, corny as it sounds, is the best policy. You're creating a domino effect if you are spinning truth down the road. That gets in the way of working as a team. It really does erode profitability. If you have a group who doesn't trust you, whether it is the project leader or the president of the company or the superintendent, you're not going to get the most out of people, and they won't respond because they don't trust you. If they don't think you're being honest with them about tasks you're setting out in front of them, then maybe they won't give their 100-percent effort, or they will protect their own hide first. You don't blame them. The net effect is it's not a very successful endeavor to put into play if you have someone leading and you are not honest about things. It's a bad spot to be in."

WHEN BEING HONEST MEANS SOMETHING TO YOU IN ALL OF YOUR DAILY INTERACTIONS WITH PEOPLE IN ALL PARTS OF YOUR LIFE, IT WILL MAKE THEM ALL BETTER."

So, when you add honest into the group of required qualities, the foundation strengthens. When being honest means something to you in all of your daily interactions with people in all parts of your life, it will make them all better. It seems simple until you face a situation where the truth hurts—whether it hurts you or hurts someone else.

3.   **Integrity**—firm adherence to a code of especially moral or artistic values: incorruptibility

The words "firm adherence" jump out to me. There's no wiggle room. So, this quality adds more strength to the foundation and is vital to becoming a successful person in all of your relationships.

A millennial says it well:

"How you are as a person, what your morals are, what your values are. I am a firm believer in doing what you say. Coming through for people, being solid and reliable, that is something I have always measured myself on. Having a lot of integrity in a lot of different ways is very important to me.

"I run into some situations where the cards are in my favor, when I can really capitalize on something and take advantage of a situation to my benefit. I feel like having integrity helps me be fair with the client. That helps gain growing relationships with people. They can trust you, and they know you will do the right thing and not take advantage of them when they are vulnerable."

A baby boomer relates this quality to turning around a business in trouble:

"Integrity is wrapped up with the other three qualities [trustworthy, honest, and ethical]. They overlap. Integrity is being known for being ethical and honest and trustworthy because there is integrity in your word and actions. People can rely upon what you're saying. If you say you're going to deliver something on June 1, it's integrity that they believe you will deliver on June 1.

"When I came to [the company], it was a great brand, but they had not delivered a lot of projects on schedule and on budget in the construction area. I was able to go around to clients with their brand and my [personal] reputation for integrity. They awarded us contracts. Within two years, I built up $60 million in fees based on that because they knew I had the integrity to deliver. They could count on it. They gave [the company] a second chance."

So, this person makes a strong case that who you are may get you in the door, get you the job. But it's your words and your actions—how you are—that really matters.

And here's a great story from a Gen Xer going back into his early career in the trades:

"If you're wobbling from one way to another and you are not solid in your position, motives, or beliefs, then you lose credibility fairly quickly. The integrity piece of it is the reinforcer to all the other things I value. I can stay strong to those beliefs and to the morals. It will help with the relationships and with the communication. If you don't have integrity, I don't think you can have effective communication. If you say one thing and are challenged on it, and then change to another and go back on what you say, your integrity is gone, your communication is gone, (and) you probably affected a relationship.

"Here's my example of integrity: I was a journeyman at this point. I had been through the schooling. I had my certification. I was confident in what I did every day. I liked to think of myself as an excellent trades-person. Working for a contractor, I discovered an issue with coating. One of the topcoats didn't bond to the primer. You could peel this thing like an orange. One corner would pull the whole thing off. I brought the issue to the contractor, and it fell to the supervisor.

"What came down from above [was], 'Touch it up lightly. We got to get it out.' I looked at who the client was. I knew we did a lot of work for them. My foreman was telling me to touch it up and get it out. Against

everything I had ever been taught that I knew was morally, ethically correct, I had been asked to more or less put a blanket on it and get rid of it. I thought, Okay, what are the repercussions down the road here? I am the one who brought this issue forward. Did I not communicate the issue properly?

"*It seemed bizarre to me that we were doing this. It did not make sense whatsoever. Most people would have just done what they were asked to do. It would have gone on a truck to the client. I worked both in the shop and in the field. I knew that the likelihood of me going out on the jobsite and dealing with the client and having to justify why it got there the way it was, was very high.*

"*I went right to the owner and said, 'I'm not doing this. This is wrong. This needs to be redone. This is not right. I can't be part of this.' I explained my position and my reasons why. He thanked me for coming in and sharing it with him. 'Yeah, I see what you're saying. Let's get that stripped off and repainted so it is done properly.'*

"*That was my integrity as a tradesperson. I couldn't let it go. If my owner would have said, 'We're doing it anyway,' okay yeah, I'm not going to be insubordinate by any means, but I was going to make sure I was heard. My reasonings were: I can't do this as a tradesperson. I have integrity. I went in there and stated my position, and I can hold fast to it within reason. I won't be insubordinate at all.*

"*If I didn't have integrity, I wouldn't have done that. I would have let it slide and done what I was asked to do. I would have fixed it up on a jobsite and put on a smile and supplied it to the customer and made it all better.*"

This story really emphasizes how embracing this quality can only produce good effects. By now, you are seeing how closely connected your qualities are. Think about what you are learning as adding color and detail to the picture that people see.

4. **Ethical**—conforming to accepted standards of conduct

Let's start with a boomer who points out the value of embracing this quality over time. Have you ever been in a conversation where someone was talked about for something they did or said years ago? This person explains being ethical this way:

"Doing the right thing. This is not always easy. Being ethical, especially in the construction industry, is important because there are a lot of people who hold that in high regard, as I feel they should. It's treating people how you want others to treat you.

"Thinking about whether it's a client or colleague or subcontractor or employee, it's something that defines who you are. If you aren't ethical or honest with people, people will recognize that. You won't end up being respected by others. You won't end up being the company or person working for that company that people want to team up with. It can affect your business because they will know.

"It's not something you can fake. You either are, or you aren't. If you make one mistake, and it's something that [makes] people go, 'That shouldn't have happened,' not that you can ever rectify or remedy that, people don't forget that. I have heard people say, 'I don't trust that person because five years ago, I had an issue with his ethics ....' I think it's important to be ethical in this business, particularly at this time in our lives as well. There are a lot of people who aren't. It's important to me."

Is right or wrong different than legal or not? It is, and this boomer learned it before beginning his career in the construction industry:

"You do the right thing even though there is nobody watching. 'Ethical' is you do the right thing even if it's legal, maybe, not to do the right thing. I'll get to that in my story. The biggest thing I'd say is if nobody is watching, you still do the right thing. There are lots of temptations in life, in business particularly. That is my basic definition.

"I was in law school. Part of the major reason I left after one year was the discussion I had with one of my professors on one of the cases we read. I said I was having trouble with the case because it didn't seem like what was ultimately decided was right. I will paraphrase what he told me. He said that my job as an attorney was not to determine what was right or wrong, but my job was to determine what was legal or not legal. That really bothered me. I thought, Why in the heck am I doing this? *That's always been in my core: do the right thing. That was one of my principles: always do the right thing. How could I be part of this whole system if I was worried about what's legal versus what's right? That was a big reason for me saying, 'I don't belong in this profession.'"*

Always is not mostly or anything less than 100 percent. This almost-lawyer has been known through his forty-five-year construction career for being 100-percent ethical. He built a very successful contracting business by embracing this quality along with other qualities that we are talking about.

Another boomer talks more about how being ethical is a must and adds another personal story:

"Being true to oneself, your beliefs. Honesty. When people approach you, they know who you are because you always stay true to your ambience [character]. You stay true to who you are. Ethics is often considered to be a legal approach as well. You follow the rules. You don't pay to play. I think if you follow your basic tenets of what is right, then you are ethical. You don't do those things. Our leadership qualities should not only be internal, but we should demonstrate them so that people will also want to behave in that same manner.

"As a female in a male-dominated industry, if you don't have this quality, it's easy to knock you down. You become questioned fairly quickly. Also, you don't learn if you don't set boundaries around what you know and what you don't know. Pretending to know more than you

do or less than you do, that puts you at a disadvantage. It goes back to integrity.

"On a business front, if your business is based on unethical practices, it enables a large number of behaviors that are not conducive to collaboration or respect from humans you work with.

"In our industry, the state and local projects are often determined by decision makers in the political realm. By that, I mean commissioners or elected officials have the purse strings for various projects. When that occurs, there is a lot of emphasis on contributions and how you support those officials and whether you get work. At our company, we made a specific decision that we do not financially support any elected officials. We are a small firm working nationally on very large, politically messy projects. We cannot afford to get into a situation where contributions would potentially raise conflicts on how and what the project should be as it moves forward. We made a conscious decision that we do not contribute. In the past, it's been difficult to hold because it means we don't win work, and [we've been] specifically told so. We still held true to that principle within our company. That's been an interesting ride.

"Along with that, we've had partners and other companies that have found themselves to be in serious trouble because of their decisions to participate in the local politics. Right, wrong, or indifferent, I have no idea. It got them in the position where they were questioned. I never want to be in that position personally, professionally, or as a company."

This conversation partner's final thoughts about the importance of being ethical as a business and the even higher stakes in bidding projects in the public sector are additional reasons to learn, understand, and keep your soft skills in your thoughts every day.

5. **Authentic**—true to one's own personality, spirit, or character

When we begin our careers, we are all apprentices. The tools may be different, but the experience is the same. As we progress in our careers, the quality of authenticity is a favorite word we choose to describe the importance of "how we are" with people in our lives. I believe this reflects the pride of individual craftsmanship that is an element to virtually every position in our industry. The word "authentic" goes hand-in-hand with qualities like "one of a kind," "unique," or "hand-crafted." It also reflects the down-to-earth idea that "what you see is what you get." Here are the thoughts of several conversation partners on what this quality means to them. The common elements are so clear.

In the words of a boomer:

"You are who you say you are. You do what you say you're going to do. You're real. There are too many fake people, not just in our industry, but too many fake people out there who pretend to be something they really aren't. I think authenticity is really who you are and acting that way. It's important because it gives you credibility. People know who you are. They know what they're going to get from you and what they're not going to get from you. Especially in our business, that's an important trait to have."

A Gen Xer says it this way:

> "AUTHENTICITY IS A FAVORITE WORD WE CHOOSE TO DESCRIBE THE IMPORTANCE OF HOW WE ARE WITH PEOPLE IN OUR LIVES."

"Be true to who you are and don't necessarily form an agenda or opinion about something. Authentic is real. It's this real persona that you have. From a leader perspective, you have to come off as being authentic and true so that you don't give off this perception that you have some ulterior motive or agenda. If you're authentic, if you're true to who you are and what you do and what you believe in, it exudes a trustworthiness that people feel comfortable about and people want to get behind. If you're authentic and they trust you, then I think that they are more likely to want to be led and to help you achieve your goals."

This boomer takes this quality all the way back to his upbringing and credits it with how he learned what being authentic means:

"It's what you see is what you get. You're not trying to portray yourself as different, as better or worse. I grew up from a humble beginning. My parents were working people. My father was an operator. My mother worked in a kitchen. I think I have those qualities in terms of a working person, who despite our positions, we have some pretty good positions, but when you get down to it, we're somebody who works hard, and we're trying to get ahead and do the right thing. Authentic and genuine.

"Some people around me, I have really good friends I grew up with, had the same upbringing, same economic status as I did. We have a couple guys who are very successful. It's amazing. If you look at them, if you look at who they are and what they accomplished, they are just the same people you grew up with. It's refreshing to know that they have done what they have been able to do and [can] still be as humble and authentic as they were when they were young and struggling."

Another boomer highlights how important this quality is to us when we are in leadership roles:

"People embrace the vision of leaders when they realize the leader is authentic. They're not just putting you on. It's all for them and not for the team. That's another part of being authentic. As a leader, people

need to know that you care about them. That's wrapped in there. They think if it's just about you, they're not going to embrace it."

So, you can see that the quality of being your authentic self is important when you are in the apprentice phase of your career, and it grows in importance as you progress and move into leadership roles.

When I talk about leadership, remember that leadership is an activity, not a label or title. You may be in the early years of your career and still have opportunities to be a leader in all you do. This quality is one that will stay with you and will improve your success throughout your life.

6. **Good Communicator**—a person who conveys information or knowledge to others

Here we are at a quality that relates to communication at last. It is so important! The way it is defined here only addresses one part of the process of communicating: the sending out of information. We will talk in Part 4 about the communication process. My conversation partners have some good thoughts to share on what it means to be a good communicator.

First, a millennial said:

"I would describe [good communication] as an oral and written quality. It doesn't necessarily have boundaries, even with nonverbal. I think all these tie into being a good communicator, being able to express your thoughts or stance on a situation and communicate it in a way that the audience understands. Depending on what that audience is, that may change the way you communicate.

"It was something I learned early on before I ever got involved in the construction industry. In my first jobs, it's not something I had. I wasn't a good communicator early on. It was a learned skill, I guess you could say, recognizing the audience and knowing that certain types of communication don't necessarily work with everybody. But it wasn't necessarily

something that I knew I had or have currently. It's something that is constantly worked on and practiced daily. It's beneficial in talking to people and getting things done."

What a great way of saying what it means to be a good communicator. The millennial highlights that communicating is a skill, which means you can get better at it with practice. Valuing this quality early in your career will widen the path to success.

By mentioning the importance of listening and asking questions, this next boomer adds the simple fact that communicating well isn't just about talking. This gets us closer to the full description of what communication is:

"Fifty percent of the problems I deal with daily have to do with bad communication but good intentions. It might be more than 50 percent. When people say communication, they often just think of the talking. They're not thinking of hearing with both ears. God gave us two ears, one mouth. There was a signal there, I think... Our industry is an environment with so many stakeholders with tons of different types of information, both technical and also business-oriented information, and detailed technical opinions that occur both from designers and builders who know how to put things together, so they [all] have their own takes. Bringing parties together, facilitating a conversation that focuses on how to get to an outcome, is such a critical element of communication that is conclusionary with results, as opposed to the most harmful types of communication that occur with our technology of 'I sent an email and shared it, but I didn't come to the conclusion.'

"I found myself in situations where there could be three parties in a meeting, and because of how those different parties communicate what they think we should do, everybody thinks they're saying something uniquely different. Yet when you start peeling the layers of the onion away, saying, 'Do you mean this by that?' all three parties are saying the same thing. It's just how you communicate it. I do find that a lot

of times, people are so caught up in their own worlds that they fail to listen. People communicate differently at times. You have to dig and ask questions to make sure we are saying the same thing."

Another boomer explains well why the quality of being a good communicator is so valuable in getting better results in a wide range of relationships:

"It's creating a vision of what we're trying to achieve and then clearly connecting with the audience so that they understand it. We're owners' representatives and we're owners' agents, and we communicate up and down and out to various audiences on complex issues. How do you do that in writing with words and pictures, orally, in a concise and clear manner? It's hard. Very few people do it well. You have to be able to explain a complex code or budget or schedule issue to a CFO or school district superintendent or high school principal, or you have to communicate to an electrical foreman why this is important to a client's or an owner's need. How do you adjust that way of communicating? It's important to clearly connect with your audience so that they understand what we're trying to do. There are a lot of ways to do that. Very few people are good at it, so it's important. I stress it with people who work for our firm. Practice verbal skills. I coach people."

7. **Good Listener**—one who listens to someone or something

I think it's interesting that this quality was mentioned nearly as many times as the quality of being a good communicator. This actually makes sense. Most folks think about communication as more about talking, public speaking. It's more than that.

It was clear from the conversations that folks appreciate this quality as important when you add the adjective "good." Good listening does relate to the part of the communication process that a lot of us don't do well.

This Gen Xer mentions two of the elements involved in the fuller description of communication—message and distractions. The message is the content, or what's being communicated. Distractions are all of the other things like noise or visual, nonverbal elements that can affect the process. An example of a distraction is looking away at an activity taking place outside the window while someone is talking to you.

This gets right to the heart of it:

"You need to listen, and you need to actively listen, not just saying you need to hear people, but you need to suspend your thoughts, suspend your judgment, not thinking about what you are going to say in response, but listen and process and contemplate what is happening, what that person is saying, what message is being sent.

"It's important because it's how you educate yourself. It's how you can keep a finger on the pulse of what's going on. Being a listener is what's going to give your perspective within your role as a leader within the organization. You can hear somebody. One of the challenges is somebody could walk into your office, and you could be in the middle of something, or you could listen to them and think you're a good listener, but you have to challenge yourself to shut down your distractions. When appropriate, you provide that feedback that you're there, you're present with them. What they have to say is what's important to you right now."

You'll see that listening is an important part of being successful at all levels, particularly as a leader. If you are early in your career, this is worthwhile to appreciate as you grow in experience and responsibility. If you are a highly experienced leader, this reminds you of your opportunity to improve results in all of your relationships. Here, a boomer talks about being in a leadership role and communicating with all kinds of folks:

"[Good communicating is] being able to communicate with your employees, being able to communicate with your client and with your team members. The way you communicate with those different people is many times different between them. Part of that is being a good listener, sitting back when you do have a conversation. I think this takes practice. I have a tendency to want to talk more. I probably talk more than I should. I have to remind myself to be quiet and listen to what they're saying and then think about how I want to respond. It's very important."

This Xer zeros in on the key point that you also need to pay attention to what is *not* being said:

"You aren't necessarily always listening to what people are verbally communicating, but you are also looking at how they communicate in their actions and deeds and how they carry themselves at different points in time throughout the day or their lives. There is a lot of nonverbal communication that happens. But you're actively listening as well. You're not talking over people. You're hearing and truly understanding and letting people get their thoughts out on what they want to say and do. Help them along after you've gathered their thoughts."

It's hard not to appreciate the way this boomer says it:

"The old saying is: 'The good Lord gave you two ears and one mouth, so you should listen twice as much as you speak.' I think it's about first of all, taking the time. It's also about the relationship building and the transactions. It's taking the time to listen and listen actively."

Listening is very, very important!

8.   **Dedicated**—devoted to a cause, ideal, or purpose

My mentor talks about doing what you love, and that's another way of talking about what dedication means—being devoted to a purpose. A boomer expands on this idea:

"*Dedicated means being part of the team and relying on each other as they rely on you. It's the old adage of 'Together, each accomplishes more.' Dedication is what builds that bond and that trust.*

"*I think it's just being committed to what you're doing and who you're doing it for and why you're doing it, not just doing it to put in eight hours and move on. It's having the pride and the dedication. These things all tie in together. It's having that ethic of wanting to stay committed to what you're doing and being proud of what you do at the end of the day. I've been here thirty-five years with the same company. That's a bit of dedication to the company and what we do and [the] people we do it with. That's all been important to me.*"

This millennial describes what dedication means in a very traditional way, a way that you will easily relate to:

"*Doing whatever it takes to get the job done. Working the long hours. Making the tough decisions. When someone comes into your office at 4:58 on a Friday afternoon and you are getting ready to go, you sit down and help answer their questions or work through the challenges they have. On these big jobs, you have a hard deadline. You want a team of people who are dedicated and are in it to win it, not just be there for a job or to collect a paycheck. They are dedicated to seeing the project open on time, to do better than the budget.*

"*We have a twenty-two-mile freeway we are constructing. We are having schedule issues. We are putting down asphalt, and we have a paving manager and an assistant. As the schedule gets compressed, they still have to put down asphalt. They have to put more down in a day. They have to work weekends, nights. It's obvious that these two individuals are dedicated to getting the job done, even with the challenges they have thrown [at them].*"

9.   **Positive**—having a good effect: favorable

If you think about the people you see daily at work and at home, it sounds like a good thing to be positive, for people to see you as a positive person. Think about how you view others. Do you notice people when they are being positive, or do you just notice the folks who are negative?

A millennial says what this quality means:

"Things definitely get tough, and we have those bad days. But knowing you will get through it, and you have people around you to help, really keeps me positive. It's tough to work with someone who always has a negative attitude.

"Every week with me [being positive] is important. I get stressed out for sure. A lot of people do. My dad told me at one point, 'Why stress about something you can't control?' That changed my attitude toward situations and staying positive. When you're positive, you're thinking a lot more clearly and not being reactive. You could be more proactive. It makes you feel better during the day. You have a better outlook on everything."

A boomer highlights the effect that being positive has on the people around you:

"Positive means always looking at things as opportunities rather than threats or issues. It is extremely important to remain positive. Every obstacle that you face, every crisis that comes your way, is truly an opportunity rather than something to focus on as a negative. Negativity breeds negativity. People don't like to be around negative influences and negative atmospheres [or] approaches.

"I think in today's environment, we find ourselves in a constant negative atmosphere. Maintaining and giving permission to people with whom you work or your friends or family to take a negative situation and turn it into a positive is worth more than anything else you can do. Let people know that looking at it differently could get you out of a

swamp or past a problem or moving forward in a way you never would have thought of before. It's truly an opportunity to learn."

Our industry is all about teams working together. Whether it's a crew of painters or the design team on a large capital project, this quality is essential to success. This Xer uses experience in sports to explain what positive means:

"Maybe [it's] how I'm wired. I played sports. It was never over until the clock hit zero. You better have a positive attitude because that shapes how you play, how you work. Glass half-full. People who are like that inspire energy. Without energy, it's hard to keep moving forward when the times get tough. You have to have people at all levels carrying that torch. When you do, you can accomplish a lot of things. I love team sports. I love watching football. Teams with this real positive attitude and confidence, that takes them past other people all the time. They can accomplish so much more."

10. Relationship Builder—the connecting or binding of participants in a relationship

The words "binding participants" are a very clear and specific way of expressing what this quality means. If you are new in the industry, you are going to learn that one key to success in your profession and in your life is relationships. In our industry, those relationships that are maintained over a long period of time are binding. Binding means they are valued and important. You want these kinds of relationships.

This millennial demonstrates that his early years in our industry have taught him to value this quality:

"In my earlier years, I was more concerned about being right and holding subcontractors and the owner to the contracts as if it were black and white, without taking into account what that would mean for longevity and getting future work with an owner or getting subcontrac-

tors to bid you for future work. Now I'm much more concentrated on relationship building and not necessarily always being right."

A boomer relates the meaning of this quality to all parts of his life. At work, good relationships are the only way great results can be delivered. In tough times, strong relationships can keep the doors of a business open as this boomer explains:

"In personal [life] and work, there are two things: your employees and the people you work for, the general contractors. In your personal life, you have to have great relationships. You teach your children to have good relationships. Here at work, you want to surround yourself with good relationships with your people. Out on the jobsite, your clients who you work with, you need to gain those relationships from the field employees all the way up to management and even ownership. You have to have those relationships when times are good and when times are bad. The relationships get you through the bad times.

> **IN TOUGH TIMES, STRONG RELATIONSHIPS CAN KEEP THE DOORS OF A BUSINESS OPEN...."**

"Back in the day when I became part-owner, it was 2009/2010, when the market was really bad. People were out there taking jobs for cheap. They were bidding more cheaply. We never pride ourselves on being the lowest bidder. Some of those relationships that I had built with our clients [enabled them to] understand that and got us through the hard times. We got work for our price and did not have to cut our price to get that work.

"Relationships are huge. You never know when you'll need them. You never know when. I built relationships when I was a superinten-

dent out in the field. Now I am an owner, and they are executives in their companies now. We kept that relationship going all along."

Another millennial explains the vital importance of this quality in these words:

"You have to love what you do and want to be successful. But you have to make people like you. You have to have a friendship and rapport and camaraderie with the people you work with. It really carries on. There are thousands of people in the world who have the hard skills and can do math and build things. How you connect with people and how you interact with them is crucial to being successful in every facet of life.

"I stressed and set a goal for myself recently to grow relationships at different levels with the general contractors, from the project engineers to the field engineers to the superintendents to the PMs and executives at all levels, because you never know when somebody is going to need something. I also might need them to need something. That's been huge."

The Next Ten Qualities

Now let's take a brief look at the next ten most frequently mentioned qualities.

11. Sincere—marked by genuineness: true

This quality is being authentic with feeling. People get the feeling that you care deeply about them. It's about them feeling valued as a person.

A boomer said it this way:

"I want the people I work with to know that I want only good things for them. I want them to see in my eyes, in my smile, and in my words that I am there for them."

What a great way of saying it. This is a quality you will see in those people in your life who are really important to you. The energy that this quality generates inspires people. This is a quality that you develop over time, but you can embrace and model it in all parts of your life.

12. **Passionate**—capable of, affected by, or expressing intense feeling

We generally see this quality in how we do things in our lives. If someone describes you as being passionate, they are seeing it in how you do your job or how much time you spend practicing casting a fishing line. This millennial's words and his experience say it well:

"I think being passionate is truly caring about what you do. I think it's really important to love what you do, not only in work, but in life with your hobbies. I think that a key to being successful is truly caring and being dedicated to whatever task you're performing and being a master of your craft.

"I am building a pretty large hotel for a client I have worked for before. One of the executives for that client actually recognized me personally for the passion I had in solving some problems. There was an incomplete design on the interior ceiling portion of this job. Nobody was really wanting to find a solution. I worked for several weeks, still am working on it. Up until 7 p.m. at night, I am trying to think of solutions and provide answers to the client. The project executive with the general contractor went to my owners and expressed gratitude for the passion that I have [in] bringing the job to where it is currently. That was something I liked."

13. **Attentive**—mindful, observant

This is a quality that is closely related to your emotional intelligence. It is about you being aware of yourself and also being aware of the other person. This boomer talks about this quality in a really practical way:

"Paying attention. Listening. Being attentive is when you're in dialogue with someone, and they know that you're listening and that you understand what they're trying to say. When you're done with that conversation, that dialogue, that interaction, you feel good that the person you were communicating with understands you and understands what you were trying to say, understands what you were feeling. Tied in with emotional intelligence, you don't have emotional intelligence if you're not attuned to whomever you're interacting with. Attentive is thinking about the other person more than yourself."

14. **Hard Working**—constantly, regularly, or habitually engaged in earnest and energetic work: industrious, diligent

This is certainly the quality that separates you in our industry. If you are in your early years, particularly in a trade, this quality is the daily expectation. If you demonstrate this quality, along with the others we've talked about, you are on a path to great success.

This millennial expresses it well:

"... being able to get the work done, not just your work, but being able to help out people, being a team player. It goes back to being ambitious, and hardworking is also not being stagnant, but it's to keep learning, becoming better."

15. **Adaptable**—capable of being or becoming adapted: versatile

This quality is more important than ever because so much is changing so rapidly. If you can't adapt to all of these changing aspects of your life at work, your future path will narrow. This is so at every phase of your career. In some ways, it's even more critical for you in mid-career as you experience the changing demographics in construction and also the growing impact of technology in the building process.

This millennial says it in a very down-to-earth way:

"It's being able to change with the environment that you are put in every day. With construction, the environment changes daily. Whether you are on a jobsite or in an office, you are dealing with different things every day, so you have to be able to adapt to each task. Tasks are constantly changing. Dealing with different people throughout the day, maybe you have one person who can speak to you calmly and reasonably, and another person will be yelling and screaming at you. Being able to adapt and maintain composure in those situations is something I would consider to be adaptable."

16. **Self-Aware**—characterized by self-awareness

This quality is not in the vocabulary for most of us. You might hear it expressed in someone saying about another person, "She could really handle herself." It means, in the simplest sense, that you are aware of what's going on with yourself emotionally. This is important when you add that you use this awareness to manage yourself so that you can get things done. We'll talk about this more a bit later.

This millennial does a good job of explaining what it means to him:

"Self-aware is when you are having a conversation; you are knowledgeable of what you're saying, how you're saying it, and how the other person is receiving it. If you are talking too much, if you need to adjust, if you say something that offends the other person, you have enough awareness of your body and mind to correct in process without them really knowing you're doing it. It's having self-awareness as a leader—are you being a leader, or are you not being a leader? What do you have to do to improve?"

17. Reasonable—not extreme or excessive

At one time or another, we've all been in a conversation with someone when he or she says something or takes a stance that prompts you to say, "You're not being reasonable." This is a quality that has a very practical benefit to building good relationships.

This boomer explains it this way:

"... expectations need to be reasonable. You can't ask somebody to do something that is out of their ability. Just don't be unfair. In a conversation when you are talking to your employees, you need to be reasonable with them and explain if they need help. Just help them along. Expectations can't be too much.

"My superintendent came to me and was complaining that some of our project managers were overstepping their boundaries and dealing [directly] with our crews that were on their jobs. We discussed in the meeting that morning, 'Let's be reasonable. The general superintendent is in charge of these people out in the field. Let's work as a team and get the people in the right positions. Don't be unreasonable. Let's not move people around unbeknownst to his knowledge, because he is in charge of these people.'"

This is a good story of what is all too often played out on jobs and projects.

18. Motivating—to provide with a motive

This quality is important from the moment you reach a point in your career when you are responsible for others, starting with crew leaders and then on to foremen and superintendents in operations. As you progress in management roles, motivating people is a quality you cannot succeed without. The ability to motivate others is another difference maker for leaders.

This boomer, speaking from a senior leadership position, explains this quality well:

"Motivating and inspiring are the two qualities that define a leader over a manager. [If] you manage something tightly, [that] means you are over it, you are getting it done yourself and by your team. But if you can motivate and inspire 2,000 people, just imagine how much more you could get accomplished than if you tried to just manage 2,000 people. Imagine if you were motivating them to do all the right things and get things done and get things done on time and on budget and safely and with quality rather than trying to manage 2,000 people. You would expire and exhaust yourself if you tried to manage them. But if you motivated them to walk through the walls of fire for you... "

The way motivating is described above highlights the simple fact that effective leaders influence many people. Managing is about organization, systems, processes, and procedures. The manager uses these to conduct the operations of the business. The leader motivates the entire organization.

19. Confident—full of conviction: certain

This quality is about knowing what you know and filling your role in such a way that it is evident to others. This begins at the trade level and is a factor that helps you progress. It also helps in building relationships.

A boomer explains what it means:

"Having that confidence ... shows when you know what you're doing and what you want to do. That confidence is felt by others. It makes you more credible. Hopefully, it's not a bunch of BS that will shoot down that credibility. If you're confident in what you're doing and how you're doing it and what you're communicating to people, that shows, and you will earn their trust. That's a huge quality to have."

20. Inspiring—having an animating or exalting effect

You might initially smile or even laugh reading the definition of this quality. But if you think about it for a moment, particularly if you have progressed in the industry and are in a leadership role, it does make sense. The qualities of a great leader couple motivating and inspiring together as you read earlier when we talked about motivating.

This Gen Xer talks about what this quality means in a way that should inspire you:

"Inspiring is bringing the passion and keeping people [around]—yourself as the leader and the others you surround yourself with on your team. There is a sense of purpose and value and regard and recognition. Inspiring is what keeps people challenged. It's what keeps your team excited about showing up to work every day. We're talking about careers. I think you want to be inspiring and provide that excitement. This excitement and newness and refreshing perspective is that we have a mission here; we have a vision here; we're adding value to our members. It's impactful. By being inspiring, that keeps people coming back to work and being excited about their jobs, their careers."

PART 3

NUTS, BOLTS, AND SOME GREAT THOUGHTS

As much as I'd like to think that I always have all the thoughts and understanding about how important soft skills are in everything I do, I don't. Maybe this is true for you, too.

I spent many hours talking with the conversation partners, then listening to the recordings of the conversations, and finally, reading the transcript of every conversation. When something was said that inspired me, I was prompted to write my reaction as a phrase or a sentence on an index card. On the pages that follow are fifty-two of these thoughts.

You'll enjoy reading them all together the first time and then come back for a weekly reminder. They are short in length and long in value.

Each thought ends with a question designed to help you remember the reason we all need to be learning about soft skills and what your soft skills are. Pause for a moment on the question, and then make it a point to share your thoughts with someone else. Talk with them about it, and help them learn more about their soft skills.

1. Soft skills are conveyed with our words and our actions.

Remember that soft skills aren't really skills. They are your qualities, traits, and attributes that people in your life see in how you relate with them and what you say. The "how" is mostly about the expression on your face, your smile, your body language. Of course, your words are also important because you can misunderstand what you see. Being described as a good communicator means that others can see and sense all of your qualities. Valuing this will only add to your success in starting, building, and maintaining good relationships. We are in an industry that continues to struggle to find ways to attract needed talent into the trades and other roles and to find ways to complete jobs or projects on time, on budget, and safely. Poor communication causes misunderstanding.

Are you a good communicator?

2. It all starts with you.

It's really simple, but at the same time, so hard to understand. If you want to grow and succeed in our industry and in your personal life, you must understand yourself. This isn't about what you know. It's about knowing you. What are your qualities? What are your strengths and weaknesses? What are you feeling?

The last question is the one we are often the least tuned into. This question is talking about emotions. Emotions are part of all of us. Our brains are "wired" to give emotion the upper hand over rational thinking. There's a lot of research that tells us that many of us are controlled by our emotions. Our ability to recognize what we are feeling throughout our day, and more importantly, what we do to manage those feelings is a must.

Are you aware of your emotions? Are you aware of the emotions of others?

3. **I am who I am and there's not much I can do about it now. Or, maybe not.**

It's true that "we are who we are" starts with who we were when we were born. This is about our genes. After that, who we become is a result of all the things we have learned and experienced in all parts of our lives. So, a boomer may say, "I can't change because I've always done it that way," but this is simply not true. This is about your willingness to change. All of us can change.

If you are early in your career, keep the importance of your ability to change in mind daily, particularly when you are talking to a boomer or an Xer. It is critical to your growth and success. If you are a boomer, your willingness to embrace change, to learn new things, to do things differently is crucial in attracting younger generations into our industry and mentoring them to grow into positions and roles to help our industry succeed.

Are you willing to change?

4. **Caring is required.**

There are two levels of caring that are worth keeping in mind. The first is the basic caring about doing the job, not just showing up, but caring about your skill at the craft and wanting to be proud of the product of your effort. This could be a high-quality paint job or a well-prepared estimate.

The second level of caring is related to how you relate to people in relationships. This is the soft skill. It's vital. We all, including management, executives, foremen, and those in the field, are in the service business, and we all serve customers. We need to behave in a way that makes it possible for others to see that you care about your customers in your words and actions. If you are well into your career, caring is the quality that is crucial to developing people and mentoring them. If you want to maintain relationships over time, you will have to care about them.

Do the people who work for and with you feel that you care about them?

5. Listening is a skill that can be improved with practice.

Of course, I know how to listen. We all think we do. But here's the thing. You've heard comments like, "I know you heard me, but I don't know if you were listening." Listening is more than just hearing what someone said. You need to be sure you understood what they meant. Listening is a skill that you can get better at. If you want someone to know you are listening, you do two things to let them know. You respond to what they said in words. You communicate to them verbally, maybe with a question. You also let them know that you are listening with visual, nonverbal communication, like eye contact, open body language, and nodding your head. I know this seems so obvious, and yet there are probably many situations in which you are involved every day when a conflict emerges because the skill of listening is not practiced well.

Do you listen actively?

6. Adapt. Don't abdicate.

As you progress through your career, it becomes more and more essential that you remain flexible, able, and willing to change how you are with the people you meet. In your job or business, having this quality can only help improve the results and outcomes of every contact. You need to be willing to learn how to build relationships with people who are very different from you. Remember that there is one fundamental thing that you have in common with every person you know. That one thing is that we are all different from one another. That should be a good thing. Unfortunately, too often it's not, and people resist the differences.

One of the biggest challenges that is growing out of the shift in generations in our industry is that we are not helping younger generations. They need your help to learn.

Are you helping others learn how to be good at what they do and better at how they are as people with other people?

7. You can teach an old dog new tricks.

Not only can you teach an old dog new tricks, it's more important than ever. Examples of new tricks can include how to use computer software to do a take-off for a job you're bidding or how to do a conference call on your smart phone. These are two hard skills that the younger generations can teach the old dogs. They're simple things really, but not for the old dog. Being willing to learn from someone who is younger than you is basic and essential. The old dogs need to be willing to learn how to give feedback to someone they supervise. This is a skill that relies heavily on soft skills. That makes it harder to learn, but it can be learned. The old dog needs to be part of the process of developing those folks who will replace him/her. At the same time, the old dog needs to learn how to get feedback from someone younger—to learn from that person and to do it with gratitude.

If you're an old dog or a young dog, are you learning new tricks or teaching them?

8.   You cannot understand me unless you understand you.

Being aware and honestly understanding yourself is difficult for a lot of us. It is mostly about our qualities and how we handle emotion in all parts of our lives. Knowing you are good at the hard skills aspects of your job is often easier than understanding what causes difficulty or conflict in your routine contact with friends, family, and people at work. I'm talking about how you are with people, about being aware of others' emotions so that you can handle yourself in a way that gets a better result. This is so important in dealing with your customers and the people you work for and with. If you don't understand yourself, it's just not reasonable to think that you can understand another person. You may be giving another person the wrong impression of you just by the expression on your face.

Do you understand you?

9.   Trust is a fragile condition.

Saying that you trust someone is much bigger than many of us realize, but we often hear this said casually. We also hear the opposite. "Firm belief," "faith," and "total confidence" are other words that evoke a sense of trust. If you are described as being trustworthy, that is saying that you did and said things over a period that reached the level of trust. So, embracing this quality for yourself with both hands will produce long and valuable relationships for you.

That's the good news. The bad news is that once you are in a relationship where trust has been achieved, you have to be sure that you stay fully aware of what you say and do so that the trust is maintained. This is a big deal. Trust is not a feeling you have. It is about your experience with another person. And don't forget it only takes a minute for trust to be broken.

Do you trust people based on your experiences with them?

10.   Love the feeling. Feel the loving.

Is there a place in the construction industry for love? You bet there is. One overall feeling you should love comes from recognizing that emotion is part of all of us. Be okay with emotions. Love the feeling you get from the great product of your hard work. Then love the feeling you get from others because you are someone they value. When someone says that you did a great job, they are not just talking about the technical part. Love is the emotion that generates the energy that leaders need to motivate and inspire those they lead. Love is the energy that fuels us to serve people at work and everywhere else.

Are you loving what you do and how you are when you are doing it?

11.   Fear closes doors.

We all face fear in all parts of our lives. This is just part of being a normal human being. The kind of fear that is important and affects you at work and everywhere else is the fear of failing. For those in the beginning of their careers in our industry, it is the quality of the product of your trade or craft or any professional work that prevents failure. Another fear you may have is being afraid to ask for help. If you don't ask, you may never get the help you need at just the time when it could make a difference for you. Therefore, mentoring must be part of who you are. Early in your career, you need to seek a mentor. Later in your career, you need to be a mentor. Our industry has done a pretty good job on the hard skills part of who we are. We've done a poor job on the soft skills part relating to how we are. We can't close the door just because we are afraid to ask for help or to offer help.

Are you afraid of asking for help?

12. Soft skills are routinely overlooked or forgotten.

If you are in the trades, you probably won't forget your tools when you go to work. If you are a project engineer, you probably won't overlook your laptop. So, why would you routinely overlook your soft skills? Probably because those who have come before you did the same. Part of the reason for this is that soft skills aren't as easy to explain and develop as hard skills. How do you teach someone to be a great person to work with or work for? The first need is to recognize that the qualities, characteristics, and behaviors of people can only be understood by paying attention to what a person does and what a person says. The ability to communicate is the key to identifying a person's soft skills. It's the key to people getting to know you. Your soft skills are absolutely the key to having greater success in your career and your life. Soft skills are the key to building relationships.

Are you overlooking soft skills?

13. Great leaders don't talk about leadership. They simply lead.

Words are only words if they are not matched with actions. Great leaders have many soft skills. It's the sum of these that makes them great. Sure, they do talk, but they don't talk about leadership; they don't talk about themselves. They talk about you. They talk about their vision for those they lead and about how to realize that vision. They talk to motivate and inspire. That's what it is to lead. The opportunity to be a leader doesn't have a minimum experience requirement. In our industry, there are leaders at all levels. We can all think about a crew leader, a project manager, or a superintendent that folks described as a great leader. Leading relies very heavily on your soft skills, while managing relies on your technical or hard skills. Hard skills are the foundation, and soft skills are the keys to leading.

Are you learning how to use your soft skills to lead?

14. Words may mean different things but produce the same result.

If you ask a group of people what the words *quality, characteristic,* or *behavior of a person* means to them, you are very likely going to get different explanations from each person. The interesting fact is that those different explanations of what a word means are all correct to the person providing the explanation. There are so many words that help us describe a person's soft skills. A solid foundation for success can be built on just the five words that are used almost interchangeably: trustworthy, honest, ethical, integrity, and authentic. The key is that the result of these words is generally the same. Of course, we are interested in seeing the result contributing to success in building relationships. Relationships are the building block for sustained success and happiness.

What are the soft skills that are most important to you, and what do they mean to you?

15. Relationships cannot be built online. Or can they?

The younger generations in our industry may not agree. Let's focus on what you can do online. The short answer is a lot. Even though our industry is really, really slow to adopt new ways of doing things, we are seeing more happening and at a faster pace. Information of all kinds can be sent between people online. Decisions can be communicated online. People can work together online with common sets of documents, can talk and see each other, can quickly deal with questions or problems that need to be solved.

But you need to be with a person to really get to know him or her. You need to see the visual, nonverbal part of communication that is by far the most significant element to be as sure as possible that you really understand, appreciate, and ultimately value each other in a relationship.

Do you take the time to see people you want to build a relationship with?

16. I know you are doing the right thing. I don't have to hope you are.

This may not have occurred to you before, but you have people in your life that you just know are going to do the right thing. The reason you know is because you know them. You really know them. You know what their soft skills are, and your experience with them has given you proof that you don't have to "hope." If you are early in your career, you need to keep in mind that it's your responsibility to get to know those you work with and for so that they can get to know you. Achieve that, and they won't need to hope. If you are later in your career, people knowing your qualities is vital to your credibility as a leader. We all need and want to do the right things. Our actions and words taken together are the way to achieve knowing. So, practicing communication in its full sense is something for all of us to keep top of mind.

Are you doing what is needed so that people know you?

17.   It's all about people.

It doesn't matter whether you're the CEO of a global construction company or a second-year apprentice; everything you do is about people. It's about the people you work for and work with. It's about the people in your family and your community. It's about the people, our customers, who we serve to be successful as a business. No customers, no business. If you feel like it's about the people, you must get to know those people, and they must get to know you. They do this by seeing how you are with them and others. They need to see your soft skills for this, not your hard skills. The hard skills are the easy part. Why? We practice hard skills so that we can get better and better over time. Soft skills are harder because we must know what our soft skills are and how to communicate them in our words and/or actions.

Are you communicating your soft skills to the people who matter?

18.   Resilience means not giving up on soft skills.

There are times when you are asked how you are with a person or people in general, and it is a real pain in the behind. The sentiment might be expressed by saying, "We don't need soft skills." When you are feeling this way, it'll require a real effort on your part not to fall into this trap. Oh, did I say feeling? Could I be talking about the role of emotions and how they affect how we are with people? I am. Being resilient is about managing your emotions so that your positive qualities are being seen by the people you are interacting with. Every day, there are challenges and difficult situations you need to work through. It could be a foreman who is just not giving you the kind of feedback you need to improve. It could be the general contractor who won't hear you out on a change order. It could be a difficult customer.

Are you aware of and managing your emotions?

19. I don't always have to be right.

I'm sure you've heard the quote "Would you rather be right or happy?" Are we saying being wrong is okay? Of course not. Being right often means feeling that you have the answer. If someone doesn't think you do, then the opportunity is to decide if it is more important for you to be right than to resolve the situation you are in or to preserve the relationship that you have with that person. I'm not saying that person thinks you are wrong. What is likely happening is about misunderstanding. Misunderstanding happens when communication is not done in a way so that there is mutual understanding. Choosing happy can occur in a couple of ways. If the situation is important, you need to take the time to get to a mutual understanding. If it's not important, then accommodating the other person and moving on is the path to happiness. This isn't always easy, but it's worth your effort.

Do you work hard to get to mutual understanding?

20. It's okay to have difficult conversations.

It's more than okay to have difficult conversations. It's necessary. If you take a moment and think about a typical day at work, you have difficult conversations every day. They can be difficult for a variety of reasons. Maybe you're not prepared for the conversation, or you feel like you are being confronted. You may not feel like you have the time for the conversation. Giving or getting feedback can be difficult for one or both people involved. A difficult conversation can be less difficult if you keep in mind that emotion plays a big role in our daily routine. Often you may react to the first words spoken by another or his or her facial expression. The conversation could begin in a calm and positive way, and then suddenly it turns into something else. Getting the best results in every conversation depends on being aware of emotions and being a good listener.

Do you work hard to be aware of emotions?

21. It's not about you.

Our industry relies on being able to meet deadlines, complete jobs or projects on time and on budget, and solve problems every day. The only way these challenges can be overcome is to work with others with the realization that success depends on good communication and good relationships. When things get difficult, some of us may take on more, or less, responsibility for what's happening. That's the time to remember that it's not about you. You need to adapt, remain flexible, and be a good listener. In every situation, the more you can do to communicate with other people the better. The idea is to think and feel about the other person whenever you can. This is valuable when you are starting to build a relationship with another person.

Are you thinking about the other person, not yourself?

22. You want to do more.

This is different from needing to do more. Needing to do more is about the job at hand. You recognize that the job isn't done, or it won't meet the standard for the trade or discipline. This demonstrates a positive quality or qualities that you possess. It could be expressed as thorough, responsible, and careful. But wanting to do more takes your responsible behavior to another level. Now you are demonstrating qualities that will separate you from others at every level of experience. You are considering more than the specific job and the hard skills involved. You are thinking about how you are doing your job and considering how you could be improving. At the trade level, you are described as hardworking and dedicated. If you are in management of a contractor, you are described as attentive, customer-focused, and caring. Leaders live in the "do more."

Do you know how to do more than just your job?

23. Emotions rule.

This is an important thing to understand. You can probably remember a time when you've gotten upset or angry on the jobsite or with someone in the office. This is just fundamental to being a person among people at work and everywhere else. Our brains are wired to give emotion the upper hand over rational thinking. It's an undeniable fact. Understanding this can change the outcome of many days at work and at home. It also points to another important understanding. We need to be aware of our emotions. We need to understand what causes us to be emotional. We also must manage our emotions so that our contact with another person is not adversely affected. It takes effort to do this. It's difficult, but the reward of learning how to manage emotion is huge and a primary reason why we are more successful.

What are you doing to be aware of your emotions and manage them?

24. I know what I mean. I'm not sure you do.

This is not a good thing at any time. The sum of these two thoughts is that there's a potential problem in communication. This is more than just not understanding the words spoken or written. Communication includes emotions or feelings. So, the meaning is the content and the feeling. If you aren't sure that the person listening gets what you mean, you need to get yourself from not sure to sure. It could simply be to check for understanding about what you are communicating and ask them to paraphrase what you said. You also need to look at yourself to see if you could do anything differently. It might be body language that distracts the person listening. If you are communicating with someone you are responsible for, use the situation to do some mentoring. Talk with him or her about communication. Focus on the skill, and emphasize listening as the key.

Are you making sure people know what you mean?

25. Hardworking is much more than just working hard.

In our industry, we hear people described as hardworking, particularly in the trades. Your first thought is the image of someone energetically performing a job. This industry is full of people who work hard. We rely on them to get our projects built on time and on budget. We rely on them to do quality work and to do so safely. Working hard may be seen in higher productivity, but our success is not just about working hard.

Hardworking is the sum of hard skills and soft skills. Hardworking means you are dedicated and reliable. It means you are a team player, a person who is good to work with and someone who helps the crew work well together. These things are all dependent on soft skills. They make the difference and help you get the best results for your customer.

Are you using your soft skills to get the job done so that the customer wants you for another project?

26. You cannot build a building without people.

We are in an industry that is labor-intensive, meaning it requires people, the people who will work together to build the building and deliver service to a customer. There are other people in addition to those on the jobsite every day. All these people need to interact with each other, some every day, some not. Interaction means communication, problem solving, relying on each other, understanding each other, knowing each other. People are different from one another. Since so many other people are involved, your ability to be successful for your customer depends in a major way on your ability to get to know those with whom you are interacting. Your qualities must be visible through your words and your actions. It's your qualities, not your hard skills, which will bring about trust over time.

Are you paying attention to how people are in addition to what they do on the job?

27. Some really smart people don't know what emotional intelligence is.

Now that sounds a little ridiculous, but it isn't. Emotional intelligence describes a part of who we are as people. It helps us understand how our brains work. Because we are emotional people, our ability to handle situations every day, including making decisions, is affected by our emotions. Emotional intelligence is the connection between the part of the brain that controls emotions and the part that is involved in rational thinking. It's most important to learn that you need to be aware of yourself first. Understanding yourself gives you the ability to understand other people. If you think that being really smart is all it takes to succeed, think again. Being aware of your emotions and others' is the key to getting better results in all that you do.

Do you understand how your emotions affect your ability to deal with people in your life?

28. The only thing we take to the grave with us is our reputation.

This may be a difficult thought if you are in the early years of your career, but it does remind you of why your soft skills are so important. If you are in the later stages of your career, it's a pretty direct reminder that all that you have done in your career and your personal life is your story. Your reputation is a direct reflection of your soft skills as seen by the people in your life. You may also be known for being very good at the hard skills involved in your job, but it's your soft skills that form your reputation. Take a moment and think about things that have been said about you. People talk about your soft skills, the qualities that you demonstrate in your actions and your words. Your success is based more on how you are with people than what you do. You have a reputation within a matter of moments as you begin your career.

Are you building your reputation?

29. It's a large industry. It's a small industry. Relationships matter.

If you're in the early years of your career in the construction industry, your view of large or small is likely based on the size of the company you work for or the size of your apprenticeship class. Our industry is a global industry. Regardless of this, it really is a small industry. No matter where you are, your path is built on the relationships that you start, build, and maintain from the very beginning of your career until you leave the industry when you retire. Relationships open doors of opportunity. Relationships are what help you in difficult times. We are in the service business. If we are successful, it means we are doing good work, and our words and behaviors create trust with our customers and the companies with which we work.

Are you building relationships every day with the people you work with and for, your customers, and others in your life?

30. Good communication builds good relationships.

You can't simply look at communication as talking, listening, writing, and reading. You need to embrace the absolute truth that communication is the ultimate core competency. It is a set of skills that, practiced every day, can be improved, and this skill set is the only path to good relationships. Some may push back and say that our customers care about the finished product of our work. Of course they do. But they also care about how we are when we are working for them. If our words and our actions demonstrate interest and caring, our customers will want to continue to do business with us. If they can't wait for our crew to get done and leave, that's not so good.

Are you practicing the skill of communication every day to get better and better at it?

31. You just kind of know...

Have you ever heard someone use these words to say something about another person? When you hear this phrase, it's usually followed by another phrase that describes a soft skill that the person is known for. It could also seem like they're saying something about a person's job-related abilities. If you pay close attention, the individual speaking is sharing his or her thoughts because of a level of involvement with another person at work. Including the words "kind of" simply recognizes that in more situations, you may not be able to be certain, so leave a little wiggle room. Look for phrases like "He'll do a great job for us," "He'll be great to have around," or "You can count on her." It's the soft skills that you are sensing that you just "kind of know" by experiencing what a person does and what a person says.

Are you remembering to notice the soft skills?

32. We all need to want to get better at serving people.

Unless you choose to live in absolute isolation on an island, every day involves interacting with people in all areas of your life. At work, success is always greater through good relationships. If you are in a position that involves supervising others, leading in your organization, or direct contact with customers, you are serving people. Getting better means staying aware of how you are seen by others and paying close attention to what you see in others. We are in the service business, and it stays that way through all levels of your career.

Apprentices, journeypersons, superintendents, project managers, engineers, executives, and others all serve customers. How you communicate with every person you are in daily contact with is the skill that helps you understand what those you serve need, and it helps you know that you are meeting their needs. It's very easy to see the connection between learning a skill and practicing a skill and how you get better at the skill. Your success in doing your job is important from your first days in our industry. You know you are doing a good job when you are given more challenging jobs and given more responsibility. Your soft skills are helping you get better.

Are you getting better at what you do and how you are when serving people?

33. Common sense is not that common.

Sometimes we say something or do something that seems to be just common sense—those things that anybody would do or say in similar situations. That seems easy enough. But hold on a minute. It's not actually that easy. In our industry, we see examples every day where common sense was nowhere in sight. Think about safety for just a minute, and you can come up with something that went wrong. Many of the regulations around safety are built on a foundation of common sense. The regulations attempt to spell out specifics, but they don't tell you what soft skills you need to use or learn more about in order to be safe. Qualities like careful, cautious, and detail-oriented come to mind. Your soft skills are words that describe your qualities, characteristics, and behaviors. They are how you are when you are doing your job.

What are your qualities that help you use common sense every day?

34. The more you know the more you know you don't know.

That's a mouthful. If you think about it, you will see that it is more about your soft skills than about your hard skills. The hard skills part relates to improving your job skills, learning about materials used, tools used, and other things. It also relates to the expected improvement in your capability as measured in production rates for trades work or meeting schedules and budgets.

The bigger opportunity is to apply this thought to the practical aspects of interacting with people while you build and maintain relationships with each individual. Keeping in mind your soft skills, the more experience you have with individuals, the more you learn about them. When they behave in a way you don't expect, you realize there was more about them that you didn't know.

What are you doing to learn more about the people you are building relationships with?

35.   Facts do matter, sort of...

In business and in life, as you face different situations, the facts relating to each situation are important. To say anything else is simply not right. You've likely heard people explaining why they did or said something, and they mention a feeling in their gut. That's a pretty casual way of saying they considered the facts in a situation but in the end relied on their instincts to decide what to do or say next. It's important to see the connection between your gut and your thinking, emotions, and your soft skills or qualities. You can even say that your gut is really about emotions and soft skills. They all play the role of making it possible for you to consider facts. Negative emotions cause problems in dealing with facts. Positive emotions are all about your good qualities and how they help you make decisions, handle problems, interact with people, and build relationships.

Do you see how your soft skills are part of your gut?

36.   Great leaders don't take credit. They give it.

Think about someone you would describe as a great leader. Think about how you, if asked, would describe that person. You might mention things about this person that are related to his or her technical or professional excellence, but most of what you'd say about the person involves soft skills. "Great" is a catch-all word. It implies many qualities conveyed in the words and actions of the leader. A question about the successes of that leader and the people he or she leads will likely not garner an answer that includes the leader's use of the word "I." That's simply because great leaders know that the way to motivate and inspire people is to talk about "we" not "I" in giving credit for successes. They are much more likely to say something like "I thank all of you for your ...." or "We won because we worked together ...." They give the credit to those they lead.

In leading, do you take credit or give credit?

37. It's about the other person.

Your success in building relationships starts with you. You must understand and embrace your soft skills so that others see a person with whom they want to have a relationship. This could be a mentor-mentee relationship at any level of experience. You must be aware of how you are seen by others. Each relationship involves two people. With a good sense of your qualities, you are prepared to build relationships with others. There are more and more potential relationships each day. Knowing yourself is a must because it gives you the ability to get to know the other person. To accomplish this, you must listen actively to what the other person says and observe how they relate to you and others over time. Hearing and seeing will help you describe the other person and improve your opportunity for a successful relationship.

Do you pay attention to the other person to build a great long-term relationship?

38. Soft skills connect generations.

One of the great opportunities to improve how our industry overcomes the challenges of recruiting and retaining a skilled workforce to fill positions of all types in the trades and disciplines is the connection that soft skills represent. People are people. Regardless of your generation, who you are as a person is the result of what you've learned and what you've experienced from birth to right now. There are differences in the experiences of the generations that are represented in our industry. There are also differences that are explained when talking about diversity, including race, gender, ethnicity, and other dimensions. Soft skills are not different from generation to generation. Describing someone as trustworthy means the same thing whether it's a baby boomer we are talking about or a millennial.

Are you connecting to other generations using soft skills or qualities?

39. How you spend your time, talent, and money says a lot about what's really important to you.

This is a very practical way to look at leadership and developing people in a complete manner that must include both hard skills and soft skills. Leaders demonstrate leadership by choosing to spend resources on developing talents and skills, including soft skills. To say that a foreman or a project manager is hardworking or a good listener touches on the soft skills they possess, and good leaders will cultivate that. Talent is about your natural abilities, what you are very good at, but these abilities can be enhanced. Developing a hard skill might be a bigger focus early in your career. Money spent on developing people, focusing their soft skills, and applying it to teamwork, mentoring, and leading is an indication of how you value soft skills in your work.

Is your time, talent, and money being spent on helping people become better people?

40. Learn from people you don't get along with.

At first this may be hard to swallow, but before you go too far, here's a thought. You don't get along with everyone. If you do, please share your secret. The fact is, we have people in our lives, particularly at work, with whom we need to maintain a relationship. It could be the architect who is highly competent and fills a technical role well but is not someone you'd have dinner with at your house. It could be a customer with whom you've had a relationship for years, but when asked about this person, you say he or she is a pain in the *ss to deal with. These two people can be learned from. Both give you the opportunity to learn more about yourself and how you are with difficult people. Learning is always worthwhile.

Are you learning from people you don't get along with?

41. Smart is not the same as knowledgeable.

At first glance, these two words may seem to be saying the same thing, but they are not. The fundamental difference is very relevant to our industry and the trades as well as other disciplines. "Smart" is more about one's intelligence, being sharp, being quick-witted, and being able to quickly understand and learn new information. "Knowledgeable" is about the accumulation of your experiences relating to your job, and more importantly, relating to your ability to understand yourself and the people with whom you have relationships. It's important to consider this difference because of the nature of our industry. Describing someone as being very knowledgeable says that the person knows a lot about the trade or discipline. This separates them from others and is very important in mentoring. Mentoring focuses primarily on hard skills. The very knowledgeable mentor has tremendous credibility.

Do you know a knowledgeable person who models strong soft skills too?

42. _____ gets done through relationships.

What word or words do you think completes this thought? If you said anything other than "everything," you may be forgetting that all of us are in an industry that continues to struggle to build projects and serve customers by working together. This also reaches much further back into how our industry finds and attracts people to the industry, particularly into the trades. From the very first moment you enter our industry and every day for your entire career, starting, building, and maintaining good relationships is fundamental to your progress, success, and happiness. A good relationship is so helpful, starting with your first instructor teaching you about your trade. The relationship that a general contractor has with subcontractors is another great example.

Do you work on starting, building, and maintaining good relationships at work and in your personal life?

43. Do what's right all day long.

Your day is chock full of opportunities to choose, to make decisions. Doing what's right in performing the hard skills that are involved in your job is straightforward. The right actions are all described in procedures, manuals, contracts, manufacturer's specifications, and other published sources.

It's more interesting to think about doing what's right regarding how you are with people you have contact with each day. This is about soft skills. Doing what's right can add time to your interaction with someone for whom you are responsible when this person is too talkative. You might be in the middle of several different issues, but you know you can't be impatient. Being how you need to be is a good use of time, even though time is a scarce commodity. Don't let getting the job done get confused with getting the job done right.

Are you doing the right things all day long?

44. Companies don't compete; people compete.

This is an idea that says a lot about the fundamental fact that we are in the service business. We serve our customers. We compete for their business. For a long time, companies have won and lost opportunities because of people. Who you propose as the project manager or the superintendent is more important than the company. The competition for customers often hinges on the lowest responsive and responsible proposal. Price is king in many ways. But your company's people matter. You put your people in the competition against other companies' people. You matter particularly if you are in a key role on the project. How you are in dealing with your customer or potential customer is a difference maker whenever the customer can select the contractor on more than just price. Your soft skills and those of your people matter.

Are you competing every day?

45. People don't leave companies; they leave people.

We've all heard the phrase that says that a company is its people—the people who own the company, run the company, and work for the company delivering services to the company's customers. If this is true, then leaving where you work today is leaving people. If you are early in your career, it is likely that you will work for several companies over time. You will likely discover that the moving around will be easier or harder for you depending on the people you work with and for. You may leave a company because of a bad relationship with someone you worked for or with. You may feel the difficulty of leaving people with whom you had built and maintained good relationships. Regardless of your years of experience or level of responsibility, people are what matters.

Are you building good relationships with good people?

46.   Soft skills are not taught in school.

The first time I heard the term "soft skills" was no more than ten years ago. The term was never talked about in any classroom. In the construction industry, most people have not heard soft skills talked about—even in today's industry. More importantly, there hasn't been recognition about what soft skills are and that they are in many ways more important than hard skills. People see the qualities, traits, and behaviors that you have and appreciate your soft skills in your actions and words. The soft skill that is fundamental to conveying all your qualities is communication. In fact, most folks say communication when you ask them what soft skills are. Qualities of people are talked about when describing a person like a great leader.

Can you teach yourself and others about soft skills?

47.   You don't get better unless you fail.

This idea is fundamental to learning, skill-building, and relationship-building. Most of us experience failing as a natural part of getting better at what we do and how we are. We get better if we use failing as a step forward and not a step backward. You can apply this to any part of your job. Think about how long it took you to get good at your job. It takes most of us some time, and we make many mistakes. It's the same process with your soft skills. Making a mistake in how we are with a person with whom we are building a relationship can be a lot more serious. Doing all that we can to get to know those we are in a relationship with is challenging if we don't think about how we are with people. Our qualities are on display. We must pay attention to what we say and do. If we make a mistake, it may break the relationship, so we need to be very aware of the other person.

Are you getting better and failing less?

48. Everybody needs a "check yourself" list.

There's no escaping the fact that every one of us would benefit from paying closer attention to what's going on around us, thinking about what is ahead of us today, and checking our feelings. Yes, I said feelings. It's managing yourself. This check gives us the opportunity to move from reacting to anticipating. For example, if we know we are going to see a person with whom we are not patient, we can remind ourselves of the importance of being patient. Patience is a soft skill. Impatience is a negative emotion. Reminding yourself involves thinking about why you are impatient with a person and what to do to manage it. Every relationship we have will be different. Remember, being different from one another is a very important thing that we all have in common. Our ability to be successful depends on building and maintaining relationships.

Are you checking yourself daily?

49. Respectfully firm is fair.

Did you have a disagreement with someone today? Chances are that you did. It may not have been a big deal, and maybe it was resolved quickly. If it was a matter of some importance, the challenge of getting the best result possible may require you to be firm in how you engage with the other person. As you grow in experience and level of responsibility, these disagreements will also grow in importance to your success. They may be more significant to the success of your company. If you are early in your career, you may feel that someone is being tough on you. It could relate to your trade or to how you are fitting in with others. In all situations where being firm is needed, being respectful is of great importance. A lack of respect will damage or destroy anything useful, constructive, or worthwhile involved. Pay attention to the look on your face and the way words are spoken.

Are you paying attention to how you talk and how you look?

50. You want to do a good job but don't know what a good job is.

This is about understanding, learning, and teaching. This is the central and most fundamental purpose of mentoring. The key to knowing what a good job is often comes down to the simple realization that you must take responsibility for knowing. The person who is teaching you may not be communicating clearly enough to help you with the task. This is a practical thought to keep in mind whenever you are getting or giving directions on the job. Too often you said you understood when you really did not. It's even more important to apply this to your soft skills. Learning more about soft skills throughout your career is the difference maker. This is about how you are—using your words and your behaviors to get to know and understand people, and in turn, those people getting to know and understand you.

Are you doing a good job of learning more about your soft skills?

51. I didn't like you, but I trusted you.

Imagine that you are involved in trying to resolve an issue that happened on a jobsite. The person you must work with to resolve the issue is sometimes rude, impatient, and generally unpleasant. You've known this person for some time. You don't like this person. The qualities of this person are the reasons why you don't like them. But your experience with this person showed you that they were always thorough, honest, and consistent in how issues were resolved. Your awareness of all of this person's qualities over time gave you the ability to focus on the qualities that were important to the issue at hand. So, you trusted them. That person may never change, but when you are aware of their positive qualities and your own qualities, you can have trust. Similar situations happen for all of us.

What do you do to understand all of a person's qualities needed for a relationship?

52. Emotional intelligence is not about how smart you are.

We all know people who are smart. Being smart doesn't mean greater success at work or in life. Knowing more about yourself in terms of emotion is more likely to contribute to your success. Emotional intelligence basically means that you understand your emotions and can manage them. It also means that you are aware of the emotions of others at work and elsewhere. There's no escaping the fact that people have emotions. It's important to know that our brains are wired to give emotions the upper hand. Emotions can be positive or negative. Negative emotions affect your ability to handle situations, deal with problems, and stay safe. Positive emotions can motivate people. Knowing yourself is the foundation of your success, and knowing others is the building block of relationships.

Do you know yourself?

Remember to come back to this part of the book regularly. The thoughts here are practical and powerful.

PART

4

DO IT YOURSELF

Now we are going to spend some time using what you've learned about soft skills and yourself, talk further about communication, complete three simple assessments, and conclude with doing some work on developing your own Soft Skills Personal Improvement Plan.

Let's review what you've already done:

- In Part 1, you took time to complete the activity that all the conversation partners completed. The result was your list of the twelve qualities that most matter to you in succeeding in your career in the construction industry and achieving happiness in your life.
- Later in Part 1, you answered the question, "If I were to ask someone who had known you for several years how they would describe you, what would they say?" You also

107

did some additional reflecting on the people who were important influences on your life. You may want to put a sticky note at the location of these items for easy reference when you do some work on your Soft Skills Personal Improvement Plan.

- In Part 3, we took a deeper dive into fifty-two examples of the words, thoughts, and ideas inspired by the conversation partners, so that you would be able to find common ground with them and gain a more thorough understanding of the soft skills themselves.

Now we are going to work on solidifying this information so that you can develop a plan of improvement for your own life and career.

About Communication—The Ultimate Core Competency

We all understand that communication is important in our lives, but that doesn't mean we are good at it. Communication isn't just talking or listening. We don't naturally connect the word "communication" to every aspect of how we behave as a person among people. We often forget that the method of communicating is vital to getting good results in interactions with others. We may not recognize that in-person verbal communication is the only method that helps you build successful, mutually beneficial relationships in business, and positive, joyful relationships in all parts of your life. Describing a person as a good communicator simply says that they possess the skill and that they convey good qualities such as being motivational, inspiring, and caring. These are the soft skills that are about how they act with people in their lives.

That is why I call communication the "ultimate core competency" and why I believe that every one of us needs to raise our awareness that communication is a competency or skill. A skill is something that we learn about and improve with practice. It's really no different than learning about how to finish drywall. Someone teaches you the skill, and you practice it to show what you've learned and continue to practice it to get better at it. Why should communication not be treated in the same way? It absolutely should, but often it is not.

Communication is core because it is involved in so many different routine things that happen every day. Communication is used for different purposes—sharing information, coordinating, making decisions, problem solving, negotiating, and conflict resolution, not to mention teaching, coaching, and mentoring. Communication's most important purpose is to get to know people and help them get to know you. This is all about building and maintaining relationships. Everything you do each day involves communication of some type.

There are four types of communication: visual, written, verbal, and nonverbal. All communication includes two key ingredients: content or message and meaning or feeling. When sharing information visually or in writing, the content may stand on its own. Most other daily purposes for communicating are more than just delivering facts to someone.

Verbal communication accounts for a very large percentage of daily activities, particularly at jobsites. Poor communication is the most significant reason for errors on jobs. When using verbal communication, you must remember that meaning or feeling is very important. This is carried in how you say the words and in your nonverbal communication, or body language. You can say the exact same words twice, emphasizing a different word the second time, and that difference, along with the signals from your body language, can convey an entirely different meaning or feeling. We all know someone who gets visibly angry without a word being spoken. You can tell they're angry just by looking at their face or their changing skin color as they turn red.

Practical Suggestions to Improve Your Skills

Let's start with this thought: everyone can learn more about communication. Every one of us needs to value communication every day. If you're early in your career, you will benefit greatly from getting to work on this now. If you are later in your career, what have you been waiting for? For all of us, the value of improving communication is so fundamental to your continued success in building relationships that it needs to be a top priority for your soft skills improvement.

So, with those thoughts in mind, here are a few suggestions to improve your skills:

1. Learn more about communication. There is an abundance of easy-to-access information, talks, online workshops, and lectures on the Internet.
2. Take a simple online assessment that will give you some useful information about your communication style. (An example is mentioned in Part 5.) Use this to prepare yourself to ask for help.
3. Talk with people who have known you over a period of time, perhaps your boss or a more experienced coworker. Tell them you are working on improving your communication skills, and ask for their help and their comments or observations on your communication style. Ask for input on what you do well and what you can improve.
4. Get involved in speaking to groups of individuals. If you are not generally comfortable with this, find a public speaking class at your local community college or join an organization like Toast-

masters. Toastmasters is a great place to practice the full range of communication in a no-pressure setting.

5. Figure out the purposes you need to accomplish with your communication, and prioritize your needs. Then find an assessment tool online that will help you learn more about what you need to do to improve. There are good tools and assessments related to each of the purposes mentioned earlier.

Active Listening Keys and Suggestions

Earlier, I had mentioned the question, "I know you heard me, but were you listening?" This question illustrates the most significant and most difficult skill to improve upon in communication: listening.

There are several reasons for this. You may be distracted by something going on around you. You may not be interested in what is being said. You may be thinking about what you are going to say as soon as the talking stops. When you use active listening skills, you are managing yourself to guard against these distractions. If you are communicating with someone, it's your responsibility to demonstrate courtesy and respect. It doesn't matter who you are communicating with, these listening skills are important to the relationship, especially if it is a newer relationship. A lack of attention to this skill will damage the opportunity to build a strong, productive relationship. If you have known the person for a while, active listening reinforces your interest in the relationship to the other person.

The keys to practicing active listening include nonverbal behaviors and verbal behaviors. Nonverbal skills start with the most important indication that you are listening—eye contact. The balance of nonverbal communication involves body language. An open posture tells the person with whom you are communicating that you are open to what he or she is saying. A head nod indicates that you are listening and understanding what is being said.

Verbal behaviors to demonstrate active listening include asking questions about what has been said. Questions can be simple yes/no questions or open-ended questions. An open-ended question requires a fuller response. Restating or paraphrasing what has been said confirms understanding. Saying things like "That makes sense," "I'd feel the same way," or "I understand why that's so important to you" tells the other person that you understand and are thinking about what they are saying.

Practicing active listening is a practical and easy activity to complete. Just get with a colleague, do some more learning about active listening together, and then have a conversation and concentrate on how you use both nonverbal and verbal behaviors. You will soon realize that the benefits of listening come about quickly, and the relationships you have at work and elsewhere will be better because you are doing more than just hearing others talk.

Understanding You—Tools to Get Some Facts

Now let's take some time to gather additional information about you and your soft skills. We are talking about the qualities, characteristics, traits, and behaviors you have. These are what people see and hear from you. This is *how* you are with people. It's all intertwined with understanding your personality, your personal outlook, and how you are just like everybody else as a person.

On the pages that follows, you will find three assessments. When added to the work you've already done, you will have some really useful information to use to put together your Soft Skills Personal Improvement Plan.

Your Personality/Behavioral Style

Your personality is how people see you. It's your soft skills on display. You've identified twelve soft skills from a total of forty words as being the most important to you. That was an interesting and perhaps challenging process. There are several more tools available to help you understand your personality further.

On the next page, you will take a few minutes to complete a brief assessment based on a model developed over 100 years ago by the psychologist William Moulton. Moulton's model came from his initial work, which led to the invention of the polygraph. He connected how we think to how we feel and how we act, and his model identified four personality types or behavioral styles: Dominance, Influence, Steadiness, and Compliance.

The assessment will take just a few minutes to complete. Enjoy learning some more about yourself!

SOFT AS STEEL

THE SURVEY
INSTRUCTIONS FOR RESPONDING

In the space provided below, identify those behaviors which are MOST-TO-LEAST characteristic of you in a work-related situation. Working one line at a time, assign "4" points to the MOST characteristic behavior; "3" to the next most characteristic; then "2"; and finally, "1" to your LEAST characteristic behavior. You will use each assigned number only once in each line.

Directing	Influencing	Steady	Cautious
Self-Certain	Optimistic	Deliberate	Restrained
Adventurous	Enthusiastic	Predictable	Logical
Decisive	Open	Patient	Analytical
Daring	Impulsive	Stabilizing	Precise
Restless	Emotional	Protective	Doubting
Competitive	Persuading	Accommodating	Curious
Assertive	Talkative	Modest	Tactful
Experimenting	Charming	Easy-Going	Consistent
Forceful	Sensitive	Sincere	Perfectionistic
TOTAL	TOTAL	TOTAL	TOTAL

1. Total the numbers in each of the four columns. Place the total number for each column in the blank at the bottom of the column.
2. Check the accuracy by adding all the columns together. When all four columns are added together, they will equal 100.

DISC

3. Plot the numbers from the total columns on page 112 on the graph to the right. For example; if the total number in the "D" column was 15, you would place the plotting point (DOT) halfway between the 14 and the16 on the graph for that dimension.

D		I		S		C
4 0		4 0		4 0		4 0
3 8		3 8		3 8		3 8
3 6		3 6		3 6		3 6
3 4		3 4		3 4		3 4
3 2		3 2		3 2		3 2
3 0		3 0		3 0		3 0
2 8		2 8		2 8		2 8
2 6		2 6		2 6		2 6
2 4		2 4		2 4		2 4
2 2		2 2		2 2		2 2
2 0		2 0		2 0		2 0
1 8		1 8		1 8		1 8
1 6		1 6		1 6		1 6
1 4		1 4		1 4		1 4
1 2		1 2		1 2		1 2
1 0		1 0		1 0		1 0

INSTRUCTIONS FOR
COUNTING AND GRAPHING

(FROM PRECEDING PAGE)

After completing your graph, circle the highest visual point. This represents your strongest behavioral characteristic. The higher your score on the graph, the more intensity you bring to this behavioral characteristic.

Using this letter, look up your behavioral style on the next page:

D = DOMINANCE

I = INFLUENCE

S = STEADINESS

C = COMPLIANCE

To get a better understanding of the result of your DISC assessment, review the following for the dimensions that were the most intense (highest on the graph you plotted with your numeric values). These descriptions are not absolute and applicable to every person who is described below, but they are common, and you may recognize yourself. Each of us can relate to one or more of the qualities mentioned and the behaviors described.

Dominance: Decisive / Aggressive / Independent / Blunt

- Takes charge of the conversation
- Rarely uses small talk
- Comes to the point quickly
- Focuses on results
- Is very self-confident
- Wears almost anything
- Is abrupt

Influence: Friendly / Talkative / Enjoys Group Activities / Positive, Optimistic

- Meets for business in a non-business setting
- Shakes hands, touches shoulder, etc.
- Smiles a lot and is "social" on the job
- Is a great small-talker
- Plays who-do-you-know
- Displays mementos

Steadiness: Consistent in Performance / Controlled / Reliable / Compatible

- Contemplates decisions for a long time
- Is most comfortable in routines
- Avoids risk
- Is conservative
- Prefers the inexpensive option
- Acts cool and reserved
- Listens well

Compliance: Accurate / Systematic / Calculating / Cautious

- Asks detailed questions
- Has a reason for everything
- Remembers names, dates, details
- Wants reassurance of quality
- Dresses correctly
- Likes a controlled atmosphere
- Is uncomfortable with sudden changes

Keep in mind that this profile of personality does not define you. It describes you in a general way and helps you understand some of the behaviors that are seen by others. Understanding this expands your opportunities to build and maintain relationships. You can also use this framework to explain what you see in others.

Your EQ—Emotional Intelligence

Emotional intelligence has been talked about and researched for decades. It provides us with another way of understanding the relationship between how we think, how we feel, and how we act. It's much more than just a connection. The simple fact is that our brains are hardwired to give emotion the upper hand over rational thinking. Since this fact is clear, we must be interested in understanding our level of emotional intelligence.

On the next page, you will find a simple assessment that will give you an indication of your level of emotional intelligence. This is a very basic assessment. There are several fuller, more robust assessments that can add further insight into this important aspect of how you are.

The result of this assessment will give you another piece of information about yourself that will help you further develop your Soft Skills Personal Improvement Plan.

EQ 'Indicator'

1. Aggressive _____ [___]
   Assertive _____ (___)

2. Ambitious_____ (___)
   Demanding _____ [___]

3. Egotistical _____ [___]
   Driving _____ (___)

4. Confrontational _____ [___]
   Decisive _____ (___)

5. Bossy_____ [___]
   Strong-willed_____ (___)

6. Warm _____ (___)
   Easily distracted _____ [___]

7. Glib _____ [___]
   Enthusiastic _____ (___)

8. Sociable _____ (___)
   Selfish_____ [___]

9. Poor Listener _____ [___]
   Persuasive _____ (___)

10. Resistant to Change _____ [___]

    Patient _____ (___)

11. Stable _____ (___)

    Passive_____ [___]

12. Unresponsive _____ [___]

    Predictable _____ (___)

13. Slow _____ [___]

    Consistent _____ (___)

14. Stubborn _____ [___]

    Good Listener _____ (___)

15. Detailed _____ (___)

    Critical _____ [___]

16. Picky_____ [___]

    Careful _____ (___)

17. Meticulous _____ (___)

    Fussy_____ [___]

18. Hard to Please _____ [___]

    Systematic_____ (___)

19. Perfectionist _____ [___]

    Neat _____ (___)

Instructions

1. Read each pair of words that could describe you in a work setting.
2. Place an "X" next to the word that *most* describes you.
3. Place a "0" next to the word the *least* describes you.
4. Please place the marks for each set of words, even if neither feels 100% descriptive.
5. When you are finished, add up the "X's that are in parenthesis (X) *only*, and enter the number on the line below.

---

17 and above: Strength to capitalize on

15–16: Strength to build on

13–14: With a little work this could be a strength

11–12: Something you should work on

10 and below: Concern you must address

Now that you've seen the implications of your score, write down any insights you might have about your EQ indicator:

I find the work of Travis Bradberry and Jean Greaves very helpful in understanding what emotional intelligence means. In their book *Emotional Intelligence 2.0*, they talk about EQ (an abbreviation for emotional intelligence) as a measurable indication of your competence in two areas—personal and social—and then they break down each competence further.

Personal competence includes two skills: self-awareness and self-management. Social competence also includes two skills: social-awareness and relationship management. Their detailed assessment is structured to give you a numerical value in each of the skills and specific strategies and activities to help you improve each of the skills. I found their approach to be put together in a way that was very understandable and helpful.

So, if the result of the brief assessment you just completed indicates you have work to do, it might be wise to focus a significant portion of your Soft Skills Personal Improvement Plan around improving your EQ. There is no denying that there is a connection between how we think and how we feel and act. Improving in this way will directly impact your level of success and happiness.

Your Mindset

Let's take a few more minutes to confirm that you are on board with all that we've talked about. It's important that you understand that soft skills are the difference maker for you in your success at work and your happiness elsewhere. In her book *Mindset*, Carol Dweck says that "... the view you adopt for yourself profoundly affects the way you lead your life." She goes on to talk in detail about two fundamental mindsets: growth and fixed. She relates your mindset to intelligence, personality, character, and many other aspects of your life. Take a couple of minutes to answer the questions on the next page.

A FEW QUESTIONS ABOUT INTELLIGENCE

Read each statement and decide whether you mostly agree with it or disagree with it, marking your answers as you go.

1. Your intelligence is something very basic about you that you can't change very much. _____
2. You can learn new things, but you can't really change how intelligent you are. _____
3. No matter how much intelligence you have, you can always change it quite a bit. _____
4. You can always substantially change how intelligent you are. _____

A FEW QUESTIONS ABOUT PERSONALITY AND CHARACTER

- You are a certain kind of person, and there is not much that can be done to really change that. _____
- No matter what kind of person you are, you can always change substantially. _____
- You can do things differently, but the important parts of who you are can't really be changed. _____
- You can always change basic things about the kind of person you are. _____

Continue to the next page for the answers.

Your answers to these questions give you some additional information about you. We've talked about hard skills versus soft skills. Those labels can be loosely applied to questions 1–4 and 5–8, respectively.

A **Fixed Mindset** individual can be described in this way:

- Believes their qualities are carved in stone
- Urgently proves themselves over and over
- Believes they only have a certain amount of intelligence, a certain personality, a certain moral character
- Motivated to prove they have a healthy dose of intelligence, personality, and moral character

A **Growth Mindset** individual can be described in these words:

- Believes their qualities are things to cultivate through effort, strategies, *and* help from others
- Believes that everyone can change and grow through application and experience
- Thinks that a person's true potential is unknown and unknowable
- Is confident that it's impossible to foresee what can be done with passion, toil, and training

It is possible to have a different mindset related to your hard skills compared to soft skills. Looking back at your answers:

- Statements 1 and 2 are the Fixed Mindset statements. So, if you mostly agree with these, then you lean toward a fixed mindset as it relates to your intelligence and other abilities. Statements 3 and 4 are Growth Mindset statements.
- Statements 5 and 7 are also Fixed Mindset statements. So, if you mostly agree with these, then you lean toward a

fixed mindset as it relates to your personality and character. Statements 6 and 8 are Growth Mindsets.

Every one of us can get better, can learn more, can be more
successful, and can be happier. The takeaway from this discussion
about mindset is the simple truth that everything about you can
continually improve, and if you focus on your soft skills, the payoff
will be huge. Then add the thought that the best way forward is
with the help of others in your work and personal life.

Your Soft Skills Personal Improvement Plan

I trust that you now know more about soft skills than you did
when you began reading this book. For some readers, it is a lot more
knowledge. For others, it is confirming what they already knew, and
then for others, this is interesting but not life-altering information.
All three outcomes are okay.

One thing I've experienced over my career in our industry is
that learning really is a lifelong journey, and more of us should
embrace it more actively. I've also experienced that the only way to
benefit from what you learn is to have a plan to use it. In the training world, one of the big criticisms is that folks go to training, sit
through a class, flip through a binder, and then leave. When they
get back to work, the binder goes on a shelf and begins collecting
dust. This reality is harsh but true. The only exception is when you
learn a hard skill that is integral to your job. If it makes sense to
you or is mandatory, then it gets incorporated, practiced, and so it
benefits your hard skills.

Unless you are incredibly disciplined, highly organized, and
focused like a laser on using what you learn, your results will be
mixed. One of the key ingredients in your development is to have
someone help you in the role of coach or mentor. This is necessary
if you are really interested in improving your soft skills.

Conventional wisdom says that good personal development plans include goals and a plan of action. The most widely recognized suggested structure for goals is referred to as SMART goals. The goal needs to be:

S—SPECIFIC

M—MEASURABLE

A—ACHIEVABLE

R—REALISTIC

T—TIME-BASED

Keep this in mind when you are writing goals you want to accomplish.

Here are a series of steps in the form of questions to guide you in preparing your Soft Skills Personal Improvement Plan. Refer to all of the work you've already done as you moved through this book; it's the primary source of information and items to include in your plan. Your answers will give you what you need to write goals and your plan of action.

- What specific things did I learn reading this book and completing the activities?
- What soft skills do I need to improve?
- What is the priority from most important to least important when ranking the skills I need to improve?
- What is my goal for each of the skills I need to improve?
- What do I need to do specifically in relation to the two to three highest-priority goals?
- What is the date by which I should complete each goal?
- What obstacles need to be overcome?
- What resources do I need?
- Who will I ask to help me as a coach or mentor to achieve my goals?
- How will I know I have accomplished my goals?

There are many different formats to document the answers to these questions in an action plan for soft skills improvement. If you want more ideas, just google it! Find one that makes sense for you, or create your own format. You just need to be sure that you use the SMART goal framework and include it in your plan.

In order to be effective, your Soft Skills Personal Improvement Plan needs to have the following GROWTH qualities:

- Goal: anchors the plan for each goal
- Realistic: to provide the opportunity for success and growth
- Outcomes: what will be different?
- Who: a coach or mentor must be involved to help with success and accountability
- Timeline: needs to be reasonable and should never be open-ended or longer than one year in length
- How: specific steps or activities to allow you to monitor progress to achievement

We've said in many places in the learning and sharing of experiences in this book that we all need to value soft skills. It should be very clear by now that they are actually more important to your growth and success than your hard skills. The balance, of course, shifts as you gain more and more experience in our industry.

It all starts with you.

It starts here.

You must do it yourself, but not alone.

You must have a mindset that will fuel your growth and development at any stage of your career.

I wish you greater success in your career and an abundance of joy in your life.

Commit to doing the work it takes to be a better you!

RECOMMENDED READING AND OTHER RESOURCES

I trust you know a bit more about yourself now that you have arrived at this page. Congratulations! Perhaps you want to learn more about the new topics we've covered. Along with your independent learning, I suggest that you do some additional work that relates to how you are with other people, with mentors, coaches, or group classes as a part of your personal development plan.

Here is a list of books and some other resources you may want to access. They have all been helpful to me in my journey of soft skills understanding and growth.

Books

Emotional Intelligence 2.0, Travis Bradberry and Jean Greaves*

Greater than Yourself, Steve Farber

Love is Just Damned Good Business, Steve Farber

Mindset, Carol Dweck

The Integrity Chain, Ralph E. James

The People Profit Connection, G. Brent Darnell

The Radical Leap, Steve Farber

The Speed of Trust, Stephen M. R. Covey

What Got You Here Won't Get You There, Marshall Goldsmith

The 7 Habits of Highly Effective People, Stephen R. Covey

*The Bradberry & Greaves book includes a very helpful and robust online assessment that can easily form the core of your soft skills personal development plan.

Other Resources

There are many resources that you can access in a full range of media. Many low-cost or free assessments can be accessed online.

There are also many assessments available for purchase. Here are a couple of examples:

What's My Communication Style? HRDQ Style Series

EISA Emotional Intelligence Skills Assessment, Pfeiffer Assessments

Search for and view YouTube videos on the many aspects of what we've talked about in this book. In short, if you want to learn more, you can find it!

Final Thoughts

My experiences tell me that...

It's not about *WHAT* you know...

It's about *HOW* you are...

With yourself, with your family, with your friends...

With the people you work for and with.

It's about starting, building, and maintaining good relationships in all parts of your life.

And this all starts with knowing yourself. Really knowing yourself!

Value differences as a positive for personal and professional success.

Learn all you can about the people you work with and for.

Communication is the "ultimate core competency" to value and improve upon every day.

There's always more to be learned...

So, continue learning all that you can about yourself, about others, about soft skills.

It is the difference maker!

Dennis Doran:
Author

D ennis Doran, a leading expert in the construction industry with more than forty years of experience, delivers powerful, actionable lessons about people and service with great energy and humor. He gets everyone engaged, keeps their interest, and establishes a connection that goes much deeper than a typical speaker, trainer, or facilitator. And while he comes from a storied career in the construction industry, his content will deliver a critical competitive advantage for anyone in any field.

There are three words that have continued to follow Dennis and capture his passion: love, people, and service. Dennis's message on the vital importance of developing and valuing soft skills is the leading topic of his seminars and the very essence of the message in his book *Soft as Steel*, written to equip readers with the tools to be successful, not just in business, but in life and relationships.

Dennis delivers speeches, workshops, and training on a range of topics associated with the vital and strategically paramount focus on soft skills—the qualities of a person that makes them good to work with, work for, and have a lasting relationship with.

Topics of Dennis's speeches and workshops include:

- *Soft as Steel*: Your Qualities Are the Difference Maker
- Greater Than Yourself (GTY): The True Leader's "Golden Rule"
- Generations & Diversity: Recruiting in the Future
- Soft Skills Are the Hardest to Learn
- Emotion Is Not Just About Feelings
- Differences Are Not a Problem
- What's Your EQ: What Does It Have to Do with Making a Profit?
- Soft Skills = Success and Profitable Relationships
- Getting Along Is More Than Just Smiling or Avoiding
- Tools for Relationship Success: Soft Skills Make the Difference
- Leading and Helping Team Members Grow: Mentoring Skills
- Negotiating Skills and Behaviors
- Personal Skills Management

Dennis has developed a framework adaptable to every organization committed to the simple thought that people are the reason we succeed in serving customers and building lasting joyful relationships in our professional and personal lives. The TFC™ framework enables an organization to sustain its success with the tools needed to do so utilizing Training, Facilitating, and Coaching. The foundation training of the framework that Dennis delivers is an eight-hour workshop entitled "Change Your Mindset; Improve Relationships." The workshop includes assessing capability, identifying development opportunities, determining future activities, and energizing each participant with the preparation of individual personal skills enrichment plans.

Dennis is a certified facilitator of the Extreme Leadership Institute and delivers a four-hour and full day workshop entitled "Extreme Leadership: Taking the Radical LEAP." Based on the work of best-selling leadership author Steve Farber, this powerful and transformational workshop explores the key tenets of the Extreme Leadership Framework—LEAP: Cultivating Love, Generating Energy, Inspiring Audacity, and Providing Proof—and guides you in applying them to your personal and professional leadership challenges.

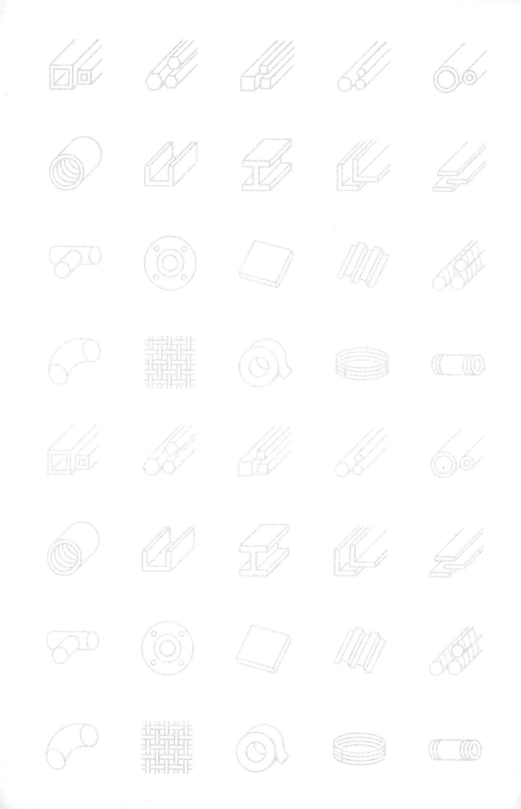

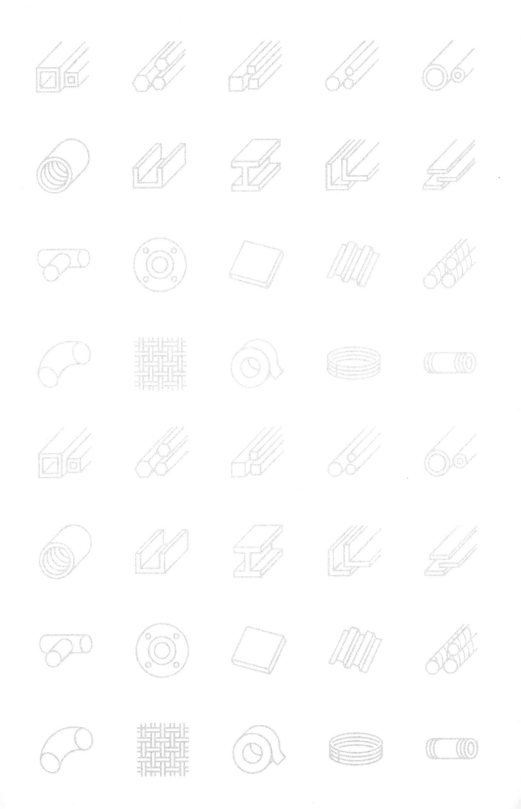

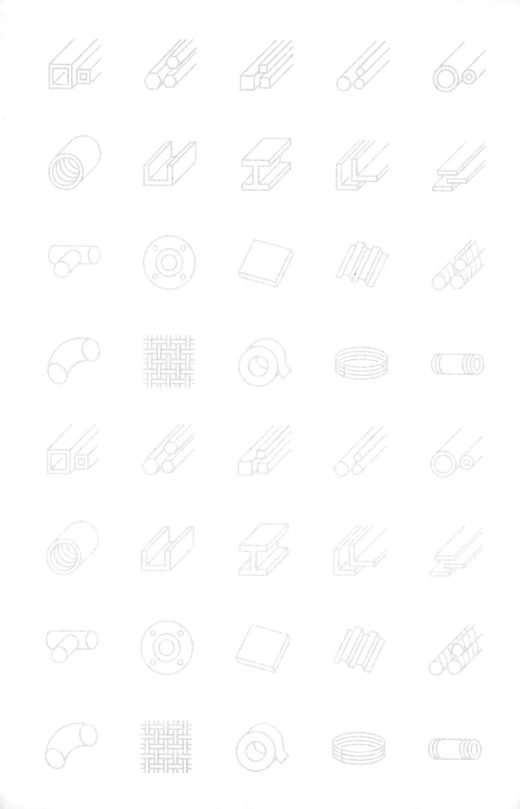